PUB

SPEAKING

Overcome Your Public Speaking Fear, Influence
People With Your Charisma and Improve Your
Persuasion Skills

(Learn Effective Communication Without Fear
& Shyness)

Joanna Avery

Published by Rob Miles

© **Joanna Avery**

All Rights Reserved

*Conversation Skills: Overcome Your Public Speaking
Fear, Influence People With Your Charisma and Improve
Your Persuasion Skills (Learn Effective Communication
Without Fear & Shyness)*

ISBN 978-1-989990-10-0

Legal & Disclaimer

The information contained in this book is not designed to replace or take the place of any form of medicine or professional medical advice. The information in this book has been provided for educational and entertainment purposes only.

The information contained in this book has been compiled from sources deemed reliable, and it is accurate to the best of the Author's knowledge; however, the Author cannot guarantee its accuracy and validity and cannot be held liable for any errors or omissions. Changes are periodically made to this book. You must consult your doctor or get professional medical advice before using any of the suggested remedies, techniques, or information in this book.

Upon using the information contained in this book, you agree to hold harmless the Author from and against any damages, costs, and expenses, including any legal fees potentially resulting from the application of any of the information provided by this guide. This disclaimer applies to any damages or injury caused by the use and application, whether directly or indirectly, of any advice or information presented, whether for breach of contract, tort, negligence, personal injury, criminal intent, or under any other cause of action.

You agree to accept all risks of using the information presented inside this book. You need to consult a professional medical practitioner in order to ensure

you are both able and healthy enough
to participate in this program.

Table of Contents

Introduction

This book contains proven steps and strategies on how to overcome one's fear and nerves when it comes to speaking in front of audience, and be able to make presentations with greater ease and confidence.

Not everyone can stand in front of a group of people – much less a large one – and deliver a speech smoothly and confidently. Some people encounter nerves and jitters and flounder while speaking; meanwhile, others completely freeze up and end up not being able to say anything at all.

Fear of speaking in public is a serious problem for many people, and this ebook aims to help you overcome your fear so that you can get your message across better and with great confidence.

Chapter 1: Overcoming Anxiety

The first step to becoming an effective public speaker is to overcome the anxiety associated with public speaking. This may sound a bit simplistic at first, but the fact is that by recognizing and addressing the feeling of anxiety itself you can begin to undo its negative influence on your performance. Most fears gain their power by making a person feel self-conscious. The more self-conscious you feel, the stronger your fears become. However, by acknowledging your fears you remove the need to hide them, thereby reducing your sense of self-consciousness. Furthermore, when you address your fears with the crowd you are speaking to you will connect with them, thus creating a sense of unity that will bring you peace of mind. This chapter will address four different ways to address and overcome the basic anxiety associated with public speaking.

Use Humor

One of the best ways to overcome anxiety of any kind is to use humor. When you laugh at something or someone, you completely disarm them, leaving them completely powerless over you. This technique has been proven in all sorts of scenarios, including overcoming bullies and others who would cause you physical or emotional harm. The bottom line is that fear feeds on fear, thus the more afraid you feel, the more afraid you will become. It's a vicious cycle, but it can easily be overcome. When you laugh in the face of fear you starve that fear of its food source, thereby weakening it to the point that it disappears altogether. Therefore, the best way to overcome your fear of public speaking is to laugh at it as much as you can.

While laughing at the idea of you making a fool of yourself can go a long way, something that can go even further is joking about your fears with the crowd itself. This may take some courage at first, but when you tell your audience that the only thing worse than public speaking, in your opinion, is a long and painful trip to the dentist you will elicit a response that changes things completely. Your audience will laugh at your joke, releasing the tension in the room and helping you to exorcize your demons by putting them on public display. Now, if you do make any mistakes of any kind you can tell the audience that the dentist is looking better and better, thereby turning embarrassment into entertainment.

Realize the Audience Sympathizes

Another effective method for overcoming anxiety is to know your enemy. In this case it might be more accurate to say know who your enemy isn't. More often than not one of the main reasons why people get anxious when speaking in public is that they imagine their audience as a group of harsh, critical judges waiting to pounce on every mistake made during the presentation. They envision the crowd erupting into howls of laughter at the first sign of stuttering, forgetfulness or misspeaking. The more a person imagines this scenario is, the more real it becomes in their mind. Even worse, the more they imagine it is, the greater their fear of the occasion becomes. In the end, this vision is not only catastrophic, it is also as far from the truth as you could possibly get.

The fact of the matter is that the vast majority of your audience members feel a great deal of sympathy for you. Most of them wouldn't trade places with you for love nor money since they dread public speaking as much as you do. While there may be a handful of jerks in the crowd who snicker at every misstep, for the most part the audience is urging you on in their hearts and minds, sending positive energy to you whether you realize it or not. Additionally, they are there to learn what you are teaching them, not to grade you on your presentation skills. Therefore they may not even recognize any mistakes you make, but even if they do they won't focus on them any more than they will on the shoes you are wearing. So relax, the crowd are actually on your side!

Visualize Your Success

There are countless books on the market that talk about the power of visualization. Whether or not you believe in such things as energy, visualization and other seemingly abstract concepts the fact is that how you see your presentation makes all the difference in the world. As mentioned earlier, if you envision yourself failing this will only serve to increase the likelihood of such failure, as well as adding to the anxiety you feel. Subsequently, visualization is a very powerful element regarding your success or failure. Once you realize this you can begin to use visualization as a tool to increase your success and reduce your stresses and fears.

The trick is to envision the very best outcome you can possibly imagine.

Needless to say, you will play the event over and over again in your mind in the days and weeks leading up to your presentation. While this can be a bad thing for most if you practice visualizing your success this can turn out to be a very positive process. Don't just visualize overall success, instead visualize individual elements of success within the big picture. For example, you can visualize that you make it through the presentation without losing your place, stuttering or the like. However, you can also visualize the crowd laughing at your jokes, adding another element of success to the picture. Take it a step further and visualize people coming up to you after the presentation congratulating you on a job well done. You can even go so far as to visualize an attractive member of the audience giving you a look of admiration, thus boosting your sense of self-worth as well as your sense of self-confidence. In the end you can turn every negative vision into one of unmeasured success wherein you come out strong, intelligent and impressive on every level.

Avoid Perfection

One of the pitfalls of public speaking is that of seeking perfection. In fact, it's the very idea of perfection that keeps countless people from ever chasing their dreams in the first place. The bottom line is that no person is perfect, no matter who they are or how talented they are. Everyone is human, and as the saying goes, "To err is human." Therefore, as long as you are a mere mortal you are bound to make mistakes. Unfortunately, the desire to be perfect can be a strong one, and the fear of not achieving that desire is what can keep a person from chasing their dreams or being their best at whatever they do. Therefore, one of the best ways to reduce and eliminate your fear of public speaking is to take away the burden of having to be perfect.

This might sound like a bit of a contradiction to the previous point of visualization, however, it really isn't. While it can be a good thing to envision a picture perfect performance, you can still tell yourself that such a result isn't actually required. Instead, just tell yourself to do the best you can. No one can ever do better than their best, so as long as you do your best you will have done enough. Again, remember that the crowd is on your side, and remember to laugh at your mistakes. When you combine these elements with rejecting the idea of perfection there is nothing left to worry about.

Chapter 2: Different Kinds of Speakers

> "There are only two types of speakers in the world. 1. The nervous and 2. Liars"

Identify your goal with speaking

Before you book your first event and open your mouth, you must know exactly what your goal is every time you speak. Keep in mind that every time you speak, you are on stage. From networking events to major conferences where you are the keynote, you must have a true end in mind.

As a speaker, you should be able to give value so that you can be valued. Every time that you speak, you want people to walk away wanting more from you. As a speaker, your goal is to be able to increase your reach and your bottom line.

I like to call this increasing your "coins and contacts." Ultimately, every time you

10

speak this is your main goal. There are many opportunities to increase your "coins and contacts." It just depends on what kind of event you are doing. If you have a workshop, your goal may be to sell programs or products.

If you are a keynote speaker at a conference, your goal may be to collect more qualified contacts. If you are at a networking event, your goal should be again to collect more contacts. Every time you open your mouth, always set a goal for what it is that you want to do.

Yes, your job as a speaker is to give value. However, keep in mind that when you impact someone, they will want to stay in touch with you in some way. You should always be valued for your value.

How about I give you an example of how to give value and be valued. I would like to start with introducing yourself at a networking event! In fact, I want to give you a free gift to show you what I normally do when I'm introducing myself at any networking event. 100% of the time, I walk away with new qualified contacts.

I know many may say this, but at a networking event I only have a few minutes, maybe seconds, to build a relationship.

So how is that classified as a speaking opportunity? Basically, every time you speak it's an opportunity to position yourself as an industry expert and to again increase your "coins and contacts." If you would like to see an example of this, simply go to Bonus.SpeakingForProfits.com and download this script that I promise will change your life.

Now that you have an example of what I mean by giving value, I would also like to help you identify that there are different kinds of speakers and you ultimately will want to decide what kind of speaker you wish to be. I would like to say that there are four main kinds of speaking styles. I will give you a detailed description of each, and then you will want to decide which you want to be. All of them are equally powerful, it just depends on what end you have in mind.

Keynotes

The keynote speaker is hired to bring in the motivation for an event. They get paid for talking and they don't make any kind of offers. An incredible keynote is someone like Les Brown. He is an incredible story teller and motivator. He is hired to speak to all kinds of organizations to motivate people into believing in themselves in all kinds of ways. Typically, the income made from keynote speakers is a one-time fee for when they actually speak. As a keynote speaker, it is your job to inspire and entertain your audience with stories and teaching points.

Pitchers

These are speakers who will come to sell a product or service from the platform. They tell stories but are also going to give a sales pitch. In most cases, you are not able to really come to someone's event and pitch high-cost products or services unless there is some kind of agreement. Generally, if someone brings you in to pitch, they will want to get a percentage of your sales in exchange for putting you in front of their network.

Most pitchers typically will host their own events. A great example of a pitcher would be Lisa Nichols. She holds events where she shares incredible stories. She also shares a lot of testimonials of clients who work with her, and in almost every case she will make an offer. There are times, however, where I have also seen Lisa Nichols as a keynote. But even then, she will still give enough value so that you will want to connect further with her, and then you may be invited to an event where she will pitch.

Pitchers will typically make their money from what speakers like to call "the back of the room." I've been to events and seen pitchers make multiple six figures with a 45-minute talk.

Donors

A donor is going to give tremendous value. However, in a lot of cases they don't really make an offer. They can be classified as a pitcher without the pitch.

Donors are exactly what they sound like. They donate their time but honestly don't really get much of a profit in return. Now if you plan to make public speaking into a platform to help you increase your bottom line, then I wouldn't recommend becoming this kind of speaker.

Many people will fall into this category because they don't want to come off as being pushy. That being said, keep in mind that the worst thing you could ever do is give someone tremendous value and then leave them hungry for more. All you are really doing is setting this person up to buy from the next person who makes the pitch. They may not even be as good as you, but because you set it up, they will make the sale.

Transformers

A transformer is a combination of a keynote and a pitcher. A person that I would put into this category would be someone like Tony Robbins. You are going to spend hundreds to thousands to see him speak, but you are also going to spend more money at his events.

I've literally seen him go and work one-on-one with people in the audience and transform them right then and there. They will tell stories. They will pitch products and services.

Even if you don't purchase the pitched items, you will still walk away with value. I believe that Les Brown and Lisa Nichols are also transformers, but I wanted to give specifics so you could identify with different types of speakers and understand what kind might suit you best.

You'll notice that with the exception of a donor, these speakers will give value and be valued. Some from the front of the stage and some from the back. Regardless of whatever style you believe you may be, you have to have a goal for what will happen when you speak.

I will say honestly that for me, it has been more profitable to make offers. I love hosting my own events, but it's not just about having fun. By hosting your own events, you will be given more opportunities where people may want you to come in to be a keynote.

Put in the time and it will pay off. Work on perfecting your craft. Develop your talks based upon your goal. Practice, Practice, Practice, and get yourself out there.

Chapter 3: Preparation

Public speaking is divided into several stages. This includes audience analysis, choosing a topic, making the contents, performance & question answer session.

Audience analysis

☐The speaker should perform audience analysis before choosing a topic for the speech. People have different interests according to their age, gender, education, type of employment, knowledge of the specific topic, personal & professional interests etc. So, it's very much important to choose the topic of your speech according to it.

☐Have good listening skills. This will help you to understand the audience demands more accurately. A good listening skill is completely different from so called 'hearing'. Hearing is a passive physiological process that involves the reaction of vibrations of your ears. On the other hand, listening is an active psychological process that involves the interpretation of what we do hear.

Keys to improve listening skills

☐To be a good listener, you (the speaker) must be prepared physically & mentally from the very first of point of the on-going conversation. Properly align your body to the audience & have eye contact with them.

☐If someone from the audience wants to speak, let them finish their respective part before you start speaking. Listen carefully & try to figure out the key message involved in their speech. If you find it difficult in understanding the message, never allow them to believe that you are not getting their point of view before they finish their part.

☐Gestures like 'tilting your head' little bit encourage the other person to have a proper conversation. While doing this, you must also have to concentrate on the key words of the speaker's question or topic.

After the person completes their part, now it's your turn to interpret the message at the very beginning. This has to be done by the keywords that you must have listened during their speech. Sometimes, it takes time to interpret all those words & to arrange the answer appropriately in your mind. In this case, you should give some time to yourself by replaying to the person with some phrases like 'this is a very good question or topic' etc.

You should give the answer appropriately according to the question. You can arrange the answer with some examples or it will be better if you can relate it with a few numbers of your own experiences.

Factors in audience analysis

Demographic factors

Age: Depending upon the majority of the age group, you should choose the topic for your speech or presentation. For example: a speech or presentation for children seems to be having more visual aids while for young adults, it will be mostly content based.

Educational level: Putting higher concepts in your speech or presentation requires higher levels of conceptual background of the audience. For an effective speech, the content should match with the level of understanding of the audience. This requires accurate audience analysis by the speaker before preparing for the speech.

Occupation: As a speaker, you should choose the topic in such a way that it gets matched with the occupation of audience. The topics which have no real connection to the audience occupation are not at all good choice for your speech.

Gender balance: Gender balance analysis is very much useful for delivering an effective speech. You must prepare your speech according to the requirement of the majority segment.

Marital status: Marital status is one more audience analysis factor in choosing the topic for public speaking. For example: a speech for an audience which has high majority of married person, topics like child care, better relationship etc. are comparatively more effective compared to other topics.

Other demographic factors include hobbies, interest, religious view, ethnic background etc. of the audience. You must keep in mind these entire factors before choosing the topic for your speech.

Situation factors

Size: Depending upon the size of the audience, you must deliver your speech appropriately. Use of microphone for a large audience is a must so that each person can listen to you. For a small group of people, your voice should be audible & clear to each &everyone.

Visibility & distraction: Each & every person in the audience must able to see your gestures, postures or any visual aids on the stage appropriately. If anything comes between you & the audience, you should remove it or you can ask the management to solve the problem as soon as possible. As a speaker, you must be aware of any other possible distractions that may arise during the time your speech. If possible, try to find out the solutions for the distractions way before the starting of your speech so that you can give the speech without any loss of concentration.

Audience space: Audience space is also one of the factors you must keep in mind in preparing & delivering your speech. If the space for the audience is not temperature controlled, they may find it difficult to maintain their concentration for a long period of time. In this scenario, you should shorten your speech & must include all the important points effectively in that period.

Choosing a topic

After the audience analysis, the next step is to choose a topic & decide what will be the purpose of your speech. You should choose a topic in which you have interest, have previous knowledge & of course in accordance with audience demands.

Choosing a narrower topic instead of whole one is very beneficial. For example: delivering a speech on 'how to improve public speaking skills' is much easier than to deliver a speech on the whole concept of 'public speaking'.

Avoid choosing any topics that the audience quite familiar with. In such topics, the audience wants to have infinite level of perfection in the contents of your speech. In addition to this, the speaker will likely to get massive amount of questions upon him & tend to lose self-confidence.

Try to choose topics in which you have good knowledge & can deliver a better speech conveying the message. Choosing a topic in which you don't have any prior experience, knowledge with a belief that those topics will make your image better; makes your speech the worst one.

☐ Avoid choosing controversial topics. Some people may appreciate your point of view while others may not.

☐ In case, when you use other person's work in your speech, make sure to write down their name, title of their publication & year of publication as well.

Methodology of selecting topics

Selection of a topic among hundreds of titles is a time consuming task, but worth it. Some speakers used to give huge amount of time just to select the appropriate topic for their respective speech. Some of the well-known methodologies for topic selection are:

☐ Brain storming
☐ Brain mapping
☐ Brain hurricane

Brainstorming

☐ Brainstorming is the process of rapid generation of ideas. It involves the exploration of creative options in a criticism free environment. It can be useful in selecting a topic among wide range of options.

The process of brain storming is very simple. Assign yourself for a small time limit to explore different ideas. Write down each one of them in separate pages. Keep writing all these ideas which come to your mind spontaneously within the assigned time limit. If your ideas still coming on after this, you can extend the time limit as well.

After you finish it up, it's the time to review those ideas one by one. Analyse each one of them & try to combine ideas of same field to produce a combined option. If two or more ideas are conceptually same, keep only one of it.

Now, choose the best one among all these options in which you can deliver your speech well enough. This selection will be based on your knowledge & available resources.

☐Take out the specific page of your chosen idea; write down all the key points for your speech. Now, you will be having a piece of paper with your chosen idea & its key points which can expand according to the requirements.

Brain mapping

☐Second approach of topic selection for your speech is the brain mapping technique. First, take a clean piece of paper & mention your concept in the centre of the page. You can draw a small picture of your concept as well.

☐Write down all the keywords related to the concept that comes to your mind spontaneously in that page. Do not write down the whole phrases instead use only the keywords. Now, draw lines that connect the keywords to the concept being drawn in the centre of the page.

☐When you run out of keywords, now start generating ideas from the written keywords. Don't be concern about the ideas which may not have any connection to the original concept at first. Just keep writing the ideas constantly & as rapidly as possible.

☐After you run out of all ideas, it's the time to connect the ideas as much as possible. Try to find out a pattern while connecting them together. If you cannot make any connections to some ideas, you must leave them as well.

☐Redraw the map again in a separate page with all the ideas & their connections. Now, you will have a piece of paper having your concept with its interconnected ideas.

☐Brain mapping is one of the most useful techniques for choosing a concept & to find out different ideas related to it. With this technique, a speaker does able to find out the necessary connections between the topics & the sub topics & can deliver an effective speech.

Brain hurricane

☐Third approach to choose a topic is the brain hurricane method. Here, the first step is to take a clean piece of paper. Write down the phrases which specifically describe a concept. After each phrase, you should write down all your ideas below related to the concept, leaving the other part of the paper blank.

Now start writing other concepts & related ideas in the blank portion & so on. After the end of the session, you will likely to have a piece of paper with numerous concepts & their related ideas. Now you can compare all these concepts & choose the best one for your speech.

Making the content

Preparing the content is the most important part of your speech. This includes preparing & collecting all the facts, statistics, opinions, theories, concepts & all other valuable points related to your topic.

It is always advisable to write down all the key points of the topic that you want to convey to the audience in a separate page. This will help you to make the whole content in an appropriate way. You should also include the illustrations, supporting stories which you will use during the speech. Using such supporting things is very useful though it should be limited so that the main content of the speech may not get lost in between them.

One of the most important parts of the content of your speech is introduction part. It is very much profitable to deliver a brief outline of your speech to the audience before the starting of the main content so that they get interested towards your speech from the very first impression.

Like the introduction part, the conclusion part should also be a remarkable one. The strategy to write all these parts will be discussed later in this book.

Points to be remember before start working on the content

Time limit

The most important factor you must keep in mind during your speech is the allotted time. You must make the content of your speech in such a way that it must get well fitted to the allotted time. On the other hand, your way of delivering the speech is also one of the important factors. If you are too slow, the speech may not cover all the important points while if you are too fast, the audience may not follow you either & loses their interest.

3 B's principle

For effective public speaking, the speaker should follow 3B's principle in making the content of the speech. The 3B's in a speech refers to Brief, body & Brevity. That is, the content of your speech should have a brief introduction with an outline, well-structured body & a brief conclusion. Avoid using such points which have no relations to the central idea of the speech.

Characteristics of a well-structured speech or presentation

☐The content should be simple. Try to avoid using complex processes/tasks or any formulae or even any complex words in which audience may find difficulties in understanding the main concept.

The various concepts/topics of the content should be in a proper order. For example: the topic & subtopics of your speech must be well recognized throughout the content. You must have proper control over the entire speech & must ensure the priority order of the topics during the speech.

Each & every topic must be well balanced too. The audience may find the speaker less knowledgeable with unbalanced content & may put dozens of questions against it.

CHAPTER 4: SPEECH DELIVERY

I. THE ENTRANCE

After memorizing your speech, you are now ready to take the stage. But, how do you do it? Here's how

The Entrance

When delivering a speech, entrance is the most important thing to consider because it's the first projection of yourself and how the audience see you depends on how you appear for the first time.

It will also affect the way you deliver your speech and its wholeness.

Here are two possible scenarios, you may experience.

If you are coming from the backstage, stand up straight, chin in, walk straight to the podium or lectern while your eyes are in the audience.

If you are coming from the front row, stand up straight, chin in, walk straight with eyes on your path; be careful with those steps going up the stage.

Upon reaching the stage, look at the audience and continue your walk towards the lectern.

ALRIGHT, YOU'RE ON THE STAGE NOW, WHAT'S NEXT?

Upon reaching the stage, here are possible scenarios again.

If you are in a speech competition: Upon reaching the stage, do not hide on the lectern as many are doing.

Instead, get off the lectern and show yourself on the center stage.

If you are in a formal event wherein you must deliver a prepared speech, stand behind the lectern while you deliver your speech or just stand on the center stage.

II. BEGINNING AND ENDING YOUR SPEECH

Beginning

Whatever manner you choose to deliver your speech, here is how you should begin.

Upon reaching the center stage, do not talk right away. I say again, do not talk right away.

Look at your LEFT, RIGHT, MIDDLE, then BREATHE... then STEP FORWARD and begin!

I call that the LRMB method which means Left – Right – Middle – Breathe.

Avoid the following expressions when you begin your speech.

Begin exactly on how you wrote your greetings and introduction and avoid the following expressions below.

Hello everyone, my topic is about...

Now, let's begin!

Begin your first word with a powerful voice and command.

How?

Speak loudly and clearly that the last person at the back could hear you.

Don't worry about those people staring at you. Just deliver your speech and they will surely love you as long as you know what you are saying.

Deliver your speech from start to finish, remember what you have memorized in the past 7 days and be confident about it.

Don't rush trying to finish your speech right away. Enjoy your moment on the stage.

Ending

The way you close your speech is as crucial as the introduction.

Avoid the expression "That's all" simply say "Thank You" and that's it!

No more, no less. Just like that!

After saying "Thank you", don't say anything even if you forgot something to say. It won't matter anyway.

The audience has already closed their ears and everything that you say does not have an effect on them.

Save it for the next speech instead.

III. HOW TO BEHAVE ON THE STAGE?

Okay, now you're at the stage to finally deliver your speech.

The way you project yourself affects the effectiveness of your delivery and how the audience would react to you whether they will believe you or ignore you.

For example, you're delivering your speech in a very soft voice with your head slightly down because you are too shy and nervous.

Your audience would feel that and they will lose interest or won't believe in you. Your behavior affects your delivery and believability?

Here are some practical suggestions:

Look at your audience. The audience is real, and they want to see you. Don't be scared to look at them in the eyes.

Don't look anywhere else like the ceiling or their heads, but look at them in the eyes.

This shows your sincerity and they will love you if you do that.

Don't rush to finish your speech. It's hard to deliver a speech in front of people, especially if it's your first time, but you have to focus and deliver it with confidence.

Don't rush to finish your speech so you could get out of the stage.

The audience will not be happy about it and they will remember you as "the guy who rushed his speech".

They will not remember anything about your speech, but you will be remembered the other way.

Stand up straight, chin in. Even if you are very scared, stand up straight, chin in and project yourself well.

This will greatly help you to become confident. Likewise, the audience will see you as confident because of your posture.

Good posture projects confidence. Try it and you will see the difference.

Avoid any form of mannerisms at all times. Focus on your speech and try not to disrupt your audience by doing unnecessary gestures.

In short, make sure to finish your speech gracefully. You have memorized it for many days and even practiced for several times, so don't disappoint yourself.

Finish your speech with grace and you will be vindicated in the end.

IV. THREE STYLES OF DELIVERY

There are different styles of speech delivery that is being done on the stage by different speakers. Different personality requires different ways of delivery for maximum effectiveness and performance.

Here are the three most common styles that are mostly if not overly used by public speakers.

Conversational. This style is commonly termed as conversational as it is designed to sound just like a normal conversational voice tone. Mostly done by TED talk and some Toastmasters speakers. Also, online teachers record their videos in a conversational tone for their students.

Poetic. This style of delivery is mostly done by politicians where they speak like they are reciting a poem.

Bombastic. This style of delivery is mostly done by preachers and persuasive speakers wherein they persuade their audience to believe what they are saying.

No matter what style of delivery you do, it's your choice, make it work for you. Know your capabilities and style for effective speech delivery.

V. FOUR TYPES OF DELIVERY

There are different types of speech delivery that is being done on the stage by different speakers.

Different personality requires different ways of delivery for maximum effectiveness and performance.

Here are the four common types that are mostly if not overly used by public speakers.

Reading from a manuscript. This type of delivery is one of the most common ways to deliver a speech by politicians using some teleprompter and other lecturers reading their presentation in front of an audience. Just read your speech in front and nothing more.

Memorized. This type of delivery is mostly done by students joining speech competitions. Memorize your speech ahead of time and deliver it in front of an audience during your time.

Impromptu. This type of delivery is sometimes done in unplanned speech and some competitions wherein contestants are given a very limited time to get his / her idea organized and then asked to deliver a speech in front of an audience.

Extemporaneous. Extemporaneous speaking is the most preferred method of delivery among many public speakers because it is a middle ground between a manuscript speech and a memorized speech. An extemporaneous speech is given from notes or a speech outline.

A speaker does not read a manuscript word for word, nor does he memorize every word. In this type of speech, the speaker uses his or her prepared notes or outline as a guide and elaborates it using his or her own words.

No matter what type of delivery you wish to do, it's your choice, make it work for you and give the best that you can. Know your capabilities and maximize it for effective speech delivery.

Chapter 5: FACE TO FACE WITH THE REALITY OF YOUR FEARS

Many psychiatrists, experts, and anxiety coaches such as David Carbonell have described the fear of public speaking as a fear that eventually blocks a professional's career growth. Some people think that there is a short cut or a magic pill that will help them get over their public speaking anxiety. Sometimes people come into a therapy session and think that it can be solved in one sitting.

Some people think that getting pet answers will solve the problem for them. Some think that reading their talks will help them conquer their fears. Some try to convince themselves that their speaking session will soon be at its close. Others even skip whole portions of their message just to get it over with. Some will simply rush through it.

These pet approaches are like drugs that only deal with the symptoms albeit for a short time but don't really cure the fear. In their effort to treat the anxiety symptoms they just hurry along with their message, they choose to ignore the audience, or they struggle in a wrestling contest with themselves to hide their fears.

Accepting and Acknowledging that You ARE Afraid

The first step is to really overcome one's anxiety and fear of public speaking is to admit to yourself that you are afraid. No more hiding behind an iron curtain, no more denying the facts, no more shunning the reality. It is time to accept the truth that you are afraid.

You will realize that there is no need to distract yourself by working on the projector during your presentation. You must come to a point where you acknowledge that you are afraid. Nevertheless you should also realize that your fear is nothing more than a thing that you have conjured up. There is nothing out there that threatening you, so why are you in a state where you are about to run? Acknowledge your fears, face it, and accept it. Once you're done with that step you're almost home free.

Keep the Show Going

We also must realize that the experience of presentation anxiety is debilitating. Once the anxiety kicks in you forget everything. At that point you must give yourself a short moment to get your bearings straight and figure out where you are in your presentation. Use a filler activity in case you get lost. A good example of such is distributing handouts that you can discuss anytime in your presentation.

Use the time distributing the handouts to let your anxiety calm down. Discuss the contents of the handouts and then figure out where you are supposed to go on in your message. This gives you a good chance to interact with your audience and calm your nerves along the way. You may even do breathing exercises while distributing the papers.

The important thing is that you acknowledge your fear, work with it, and allow it to dissipate. Take note that it will dissipate eventually like a huge wave that comes and eventually goes away. Keep the show going and wait for the adrenaline to wash away as the presentation continues.

Treating it like a Fever

What do you do when you have a fever? Most folks will take their temperature to confirm that they have a fever and then take fever reducing medication like Tylenol or something. But does that really cure you?

A fever is actually just a symptom of a disease. In fact a fever is a good sign. It means that your body can react to disease and fight it. Fever reducing medication does not cure the disease. It only makes you feel more comfortable. The fever will go away on its own eventually. Your body will handle it.

The same is true when you get an anxiety attack. It's a perfectly normal symptom or reaction of your body. Your body will handle the anxiety on its own and it will go away eventually. The important thing is that you facilitate your comfort as the symptoms pass away. One way to do that is to do perform breathing exercises.

Take note that these breathing exercises are helps. They are not necessarily the cure to any anxiety induced situation.

Chapter 6: Structure and Body of a Sermon

There are two concepts that I want you to understand when you are getting ready to write out a Sermon. The first concept is called 'Sermon Structure.' This is explained as a guide or a form you will use to deliver the message you have prepared. The second concept is called 'Sermon Body.' This is explained as the message you have to deliver. These are two concepts that go hand in hand when public speaking. What have you prepared, and how will you deliver it.

Sermon Structure

Sermon Structure is dependent upon the expectation that is being asked of you. Here are some Examples:

Example 1: Sermon Structure for Bible Study

Topic:

Verse:

Personal thoughts:

Cross-references found:

Discussion questions:

Thoughts from the group:

Example 2: Sermon Structure for personal Testimony

Prayer:

Life before Jesus:

How you become a Christian:

What life is like with Jesus:

Favorite verse / closing prayer:

Example 3: Sermon Structure to Preach a Sermon

Opening prayer:

Topic:

Scripture:

Point 1:

Scripture:

Point 2:

Scripture:

Point 3:

Scripture:

Personal application / Questions:

There are many different ways to develop Sermon Structure. Understanding the expectation is the most important thing when developing a structure to follow.

Sermon Body with 3 ready to use examples:

What you have prepared and researched is the body of your sermon. Sermon Body should be three simple things:

Scripture

Research

Personal application

What is the Scripture you are using? How can you explain your research? How can people apply the Scripture to their life or what is being learnt? That's it. It sounds quite simple but answering these three questions is a very long process that you will learn.

Here are some examples using the one Bible passage three different ways using the Sermon Structure examples that were given.

Example 1: Sermon Structure for Bible Study

Topic: Learning to live a life that is blessed.

Verse: Psalm 1:1-3 (New International Version) "Blessed is the one who does not walk in the steps of the wicked or stand in the way that sinners take of sit in the company of mockers but whose delight is in the law of the Lord, and who meditates on his law day and night. That person is like a tree planted by streams of water, which yields its fruit in season and whose leaf does not wither – whatever they do prospers."

Personal thoughts: My personal thoughts are taken from the first Verse in this passage. It first says that we shouldn't walk in the steps of the wicked. That means following bad people or doing things that we know are bad. The second thing that this Verse says is that we shouldn't stand in the way of sinners. This means we shouldn't entertain friends that choose to live in sin. The last thing this Verse says is to not sit in the company of mockers. Some Versions say complainers or gossipers. This means we shouldn't spread gossip or make fun of people.

Cross-references found: Ephesians 4:32 (New International Version) "Be kind and compassionate to one another, forgiving each other, just as in Christ God forgave you."

Discussion questions: How should we act to people around us? When we hear someone talking negatively about someone else, how should we respond? If we have a problem with someone, how should we treat that person?

Thoughts from the group: Personal

Example 2: Sermon Structure for personal Testimony

Prayer: Dear God, please help me share my testimony. Thank you for saving me. Amen

Life before Jesus: Life before Jesus was rough. I was living for myself and I had a hard time thinking about others.

How you become a Christian: Someone from my Church prayed with me.

What life is like with Jesus: Life is still hard but I have Jesus in my heart and I know that I am living for him.

Favorite verse / closing prayer: A favorite Bible Verse is Psalm 1:3 (New International Version) "That person is like a tree planted by streams of water, which yields its fruit in season and whose leaf does not wither — whatever they do prospers." This Verse talks about the benefits of people who choose to live a godly life.

Example 3: Sermon Structure to Preach a Sermon

Opening prayer: Thank you Jesus for today. Please help me preach and talk about what I have studied. Amen

Topic: Choosing to do what is good, and getting rewarded.

Point 1: The Bible says I am blessed when I don't follow bad people. My friends should be on the same path I am on.

Scripture: Psalm 1:1 (New International Version) "Blessed is the one who does not walk in the steps of the wicked or stand in the way that sinners take or sit in the company of mockers."

Point 2: The Bible says I am blessed when I read and meditate on the Bible.

Scripture: Psalm 1:2 (New International Version) "But whose delight in the law of the Lord, and who meditates on his law day and night."

Point 3: The Bible says that whatever I do will prosper when it comes to drawing close to God.

Scripture: Psalm 1:3 (New International Version) "That person is like a tree planted by streams of water, which yields its fruit in season and whose leaf does not whither – whatever they do prospers."

Personal application / Questions: When we choose to do what is good we are blessed. Are there things in your life that you know are wrong but you still do them? Is there a way you can talk to someone about friends that are a bad influence in your life? What are some steps you can take when you are around people that you know you shouldn't be?

Chapter 7: Successful Research and Why Public Speaking Matters More Than Ever

How to successfully research

Normally when you plan to give a speech, you will already have a good basic knowledge of the topic or you would not have been asked in the first place, but this is not always the case. There are other factors to take into consideration. For instance, perhaps you have been asked to do a talk but with a given time frame. You may know the topic well enough, but the time slot is longer than you are comfortable with. More research would be necessary to make sure you are able to comfortably cover the timing.

It is possible to be asked to do a speech where the topic is outside of your normal experiences and this can happen in work conferences where someone has pulled out or is not available and you have been asked to stand in. This thought alone could spark off nerves and that would be perfectly normal. However, it is only the fear of not knowing the topic thoroughly enough that is causing fear. This can be put right through research.

Tip

Knowing your audience is essential, as this will give you a grounding on how much depth you will need.

The Internet has changed our lives where knowledge is concerned. Almost every topic is covered, and it offers a wealth of knowledge right at our fingertips. However, when researching for use within a script, it is important to be careful as there are a lot of incorrect facts published online.

If a site is an authority site, then, it has a better chance of its content being factual. It would still be best to check several sites to endorse the information given to be sure. The Internet is an extremely valuable tool for research and there may even be speeches published on subjects such as yours which can be tweaked and made your own if you are not confident at script writing.

There is still something special about doing research in a library. It may just be that feeling of nostalgia or that there is still the human touch, as there are people working there who can guide you to the right section for your research topic. The library also has similar research methods as the Internet with their database loaded onto computers. This is useful if you are looking for a particular publication. The local library would have once been the place to do most of your research, but the Internet has changed this completely, but it still has its uses and contains a wealth of information. The ambience of a library makes working on research a very comfortable proposition.

When trying to find facts to support your script, you should consider magazines as a source of research depending on the script topic. Most of the big newsagents will have something relevant. It may not be the best option as a starting point but can help to add statistics or may contain information which provides you with ideas. Research can be fun, and it is a great way to absorb more information on a topic. Even if you know the subject well you would be surprised at the amount of ideas a little research can spring up.

Why Public Speaking is So Important.

Public speaking enables you to engage an audience. It's an important role especially if you are talking about a subject that means a lot to you. Even if you have been asked to give a speech at work, you still have the opportunity to provide accurate and well-researched information and to present it in a way that engages your audience.

Public speaking enables the intimacy of being in front of your audience and of being able to see their reactions to your words. Body language and voice tone all play a part in getting the audience on your side. Politicians are masters at this. They can sway an audience with their words even if they are not strictly telling the truth. Public speaking is a very powerful way of communicating. Public speaking can help you climb the corporate ladder in ways that hard work alone can't do. It gets you noticed, you get noticed as a confident person who can present to colleagues of any level. You get to build powerful connections as people listen, observe and take notes.

Public speaking can be the building block to promotion or, to start up as a professional public speaker. It can transform you into a dynamic and confident person who naturally gets things done. These are the very traits that are likely to help you climb the success ladder. People quickly notice these elements in others.

Chapter 8: The Public Speaking Blueprint

What you are going to learn here is 18 years in the making. It's my pride and joy, and I have taught it to thousands of different people now. This is literally the framework, blueprint, skeleton, key, or whatever you want to call it, to effective public speaking.

In the past, I thought effective was different, depending on the talk or presentation. The fact is it's always the same it's how well you can sell your idea. Do that well enough and the action you want to take is secondary.

Martin Luther King was trying to create a human rights movement. First, he had to sell his dream.

The great real estate agents of the world don't try and sell you a home; they sell you the idea of what it would be like to live in there, start a family, or grow old in it. The same goes for pitching to investors, tendering for a project, teaching a classroom, or motivating a sports side.

Sell the idea and the results will follow.

The thing about an idea is its future based. I'm not American and do not have any real political stance when it comes to the President of the United States. As a marketer, I was, however, interested when I heard the common theme around what has made successful presidential campaigns over the past hundred years.

It's selling a future based idea. Go back and look at the previous elections, and you will see this rings true. When you compare the most recent election Trump vs Clinton this is evident.

Living in Australia, I've had this discussion with a lot of people. I ask them what Trump stood for in his campaign. Most quickly reply "Make America Great Again". He managed to get that message into the brains of people all over the world.

People can relate because most can cast their minds back to a time when certain things were better. This doesn't mean it's true, but that doesn't matter in this case.

Think back, and lots of aspects of life were harder, there was still a financial crisis, job shortages, education and health funding issues, and complaints about tax and immigration.

The thing was, he created was an image in people's heads that allowed them to future pace (imagine a future), based on their own personal favourite times in the past, and escape from whatever is troubling them now. Ask the same for Clinton.... most don't know. It was "Stronger Together".

I won't go into my interpretation of it, apart from to say it highlights a lot regarding the here and now, rather than creating an image of the future to get excited about.

When we present it is critical to understand we are selling an idea based on the future. If you can sell that, everything else you want from the presentation will fall into line. To do this effectively you need the Public Speaking Blueprint.

You can literally take this and no matter your preparation time, the time you must speak for, or the type of presentation you have to give; if you implement it, you will come across as a charismatic, engaging, entertaining and most of all memorable speaker.

I've used this framework for eulogies, 21st birthday speeches, wedding toasts, and solo podcast episodes; all the way to ted talks, keynote presentations, and big boardroom pitches.

This will work for you to in any situation!

Overcoming fear is an important aspect to ensure you can implement this effectively. Even though we just dealt with fear, some of your brains are still trying to find excuses as to why you should be frightened and avoid public speaking.

As I said previously, when we reframe fear and add a blueprint to success, it's no longer a fear; it's just an opportunity to live our best life. The Public Speaking Blueprint is where the rubber meets the road!

The first part of the public speaking blueprint involves giving away something. Burning it actually.

You collectively need to burn your figurative security blanket. You know; the things babies have to remind themselves they feel safe and protected.

This blanket is your cue cards.

I need you to understand that they are doing your brand, business, and self a disservice by using them. They ruin any rapports, change your body language, and result in you not being present in the moment.

Worst of all is that they are a massive time waster. They waste my time, your time, and everyone in the audience's time. We have all been in the audience when the speaker walks out on stage and spends the next 15 minutes looking up at the audience with an awkward smile at the end of every sentence.

Let's be honest; you'd might as well just send me a word document with your talk, as I could have read the essay much quicker than you read it.

When we sit in an audience, boardroom, or training seminar, we are giving up our most valuable asset – time. We have not come to listen to you read off small sheets of paper. We have come to be entertained, to be wowed, to be taken on a journey, and have an idea planted in our minds.

I know you out there are thinking 'ah but I don't use cue cards, I always present off slides'.

Great!

Before you drink too much of your own Kool-Aid, answer me this; do you read any more than 10% of your presentation off them?

Most talks I see, 60-80% is read off the slides. If this is all you have done, you just progressed to a digital cue card, or as it is commonly referred to; death by PowerPoint.

Slides should be an aid to a presentation; not the presentation itself.

There is one other speaking style out there that a small percentage of you belong to. This style is one many think all the best speakers use.

This sticks out just as much as cue cards and death by PowerPoint; and the longer your talk, the less likely you will be able to do it.

It's the dreaded memorizer.

I don't know about you, but I have trouble remembering what I had for lunch, where I left my keys, and what day of the week it is. Good luck trying to remember word for word a keynote presentation or pitch that could last 90 minutes plus.

I have seen speakers who have tried this and got lost, frozen, and let all their worst fears come true in the bright lights and big audiences. At a TEDx event, I spoke to one of the other speakers who was a well-respected lecturer but was nearly cut from the program because they had written and failed to memorize their talk. In the rehearsal, they lost their place in their head. Cue what felt like an eternity frozen on stage, running through virtual notes in their head.

Memorization is not the way forward.

It's a lot more harmful than you think. It's kind of like black ice; everything is going fine, and then suddenly you can't remember what comes next, your heart starts racing, your brain goes blank, and everything is spiralling out of control.

Extemporaneous speaking is.

Although the word looks somewhat made up it, means to be carefully prepare a speech but then to deliver it without notes or 'off the cuff'.

I'm sure if we were to meet face to face at a coffee shop, we would both be able to hold a conversation one to one easily. We speak from what we know and conversation flows. As soon as we stand up in front of a group however, and try and read or recite from memory, we turn to a stuttering, trembling mess.

So why do we do it? Why do we try and memorize a talk, turn into a stuttering mess, or end up sounding like a robot?

The reality we must understand is that nine times out of ten, we are the subject matter expert in the room. We know more about the topic than others. We have been given the opportunity to speak to educate, inform, and entertain the audience. I mean that's the reason we are up there, isn't it?

We know what we are there to talk about, so why we don't just treat it like a conversation and speak off the points we know?

While I let that sink in here's a little AHA moment for you. Besides freezing up on stage, most people's second biggest fear when presenting is forgetting an important point.

Something that has served many of my students over the years; even if you forget something, guess what…. No one else in the audience knows you have missed it. It's not the end of the world. If people don't know, it probably doesn't matter.

In the past, I have forgotten things that I thought was a key fact, statistic, or point I wanted to make. I was still congratulated about my presentation after the fact. People still got value. There was still a positive impact made.

Alright, Victor, so let me get this straight; to become a confident speaker, I can jot down a few key points and speak about each of them?

Yup!

What you are about to learn though will make it even easier and applicable, even when you aren't the expert in the room or expertise isn't needed.

I want you to keep in mind for the rest of this book as I introduce to The Public Speaking Blueprint, you are, from now on, only speaking from key points. Close your PowerPoint, for now, burn those cue cards, and give your brain the day off from trying to memorize complex things that you already know.

This framework will challenge many of the myths you have been sold over the years when it comes to Public Speaking. That's ok. Trust the process.

This is based off 'Pareto's Law' or as some others know it the 80/20 method. I was introduced to this by Tim Ferris in his book, "The Four-Hour Work Week".

The law comes after Vilfredo Pareto noticed over a hundred years ago that 80% of the yield of his tomatoes came from 20% of his plants. He then started looking at all aspects of life and quickly saw that 80% of the results can be achieved with 20% of the effort and the final 20% takes significantly more work (the other 80%).

For this blueprint, we will be looking to be better than 80% of other speakers, with only 20% of the effort. In the second half of this book, we will explore how to be in the top 1% of speakers.

Introducing "The Public Speaking Blueprint". The culmination of 18 years of speaking, teaching, learning, and experimenting.

Once learnt, you can use the blueprint for a 3-minute chat to your staff, all the way up to multiple day trainings you may run. The preparation time will no longer be a worry, the setting and style of the talk irrelevant, and the audience size will never phase you. You will save time preparing your talks, be more confident in delivering them, convey a more effective message, and have more fun doing it.

To start you need to be crystal clear on your one overarching message.

What is the one message, when you finish, that you want the audience to walk away with and immediately act on from your talk? When it comes to getting clear on this, don't start to get bogged down on any finer details. This isn't a statistic or a benefit or feature. Your one overarching message is what your entire speech is built on. Take for instance one of my favourite talks; Martin Luther King's "I have a dream".

Apart from the clear title, when you listen to it, you walk away with the overarching message that he has a dream for all to live in a world of equality. All the rest of his points, his analogies, and his stories drive this home. If the huge crowd walked away with that, he has succeeded. All of the smaller details aid this cause but don't define his speech.

I would highly recommend you jump on YouTube and spend the 17 minutes watching this talk, as there are a lot of brilliant techniques interwoven within his talk. He takes the audience on a journey from the past, to the current situation, and then leading them into a future-based cause of his dream. He uses repetition of certain words and sayings to reconnect the current point with the overarching message.

The overarching message in a talk is built up with the different points a speaker makes within a presentation. Usually, this is 2-3 key points to highlight logically or emotively your message. Most speakers, however, lose people before they even get to the points within the speech.

Tell me if this sounds familiar; a speaker is introduced onto the stage and begins with "Hi my name's John and today I'm going to be talking to you about..." blah blah blah. This creates a snooze fest from the start. You need to entertain and engage people and take them on a journey.

An important lesson I have learnt in business that applies to speaking as well, is the concept of 'What's in it for me?".

It's human nature for people to care more about themselves than you.

Too often we centre our presentations around ourselves. Show your audience what's in it for them, gain rapport, and then you will have control of the narrative.

Watch all the best motivational, educational, and particularly humorous talks you can, and you will see this is done the same way time after time. With a story. A story starts to draw a picture in people's heads. It allows you to pre-frame the audience with a thought. It sets the framework for the talk and lets you control the journey.

As humans we love to be in control; we love to think we know where things are going, and to have a sense of predictability. The audience's brains want to automatically fill in the gaps to any unknowns. When you control the narrative and don't let the cat out of the bag, then it keeps people engaged. This story is going to be different depending on the type of talk, but the premise is the same.

We go deeper into storytelling in the next section, but in the meantime, I want you to start thinking of some of your favourite movies and how they did this.

"The Sixth Sense", "Fight Club", and "A Beautiful Mind" do this brilliantly. They take you in one direction, you think you have some idea where it's going them BOOM... Plot twist!

This is where you want your stories and subsequently your presentations to go. Craft your stories to create intrigue, get the audience gripping onto to your next word, and your message will be 10x better received.

Creating a compelling story or analogy prequalifies your audience. They know if the rest of the talk is for them or not. Providing you know your audience, this should be everyone present. This is asking permission before you serve up the main course. If done well, you don't only have them giving permission, but begging for more.

This allows you then to flow into your next 2- 3 points. The reason I say flow is because they should be like a waterfall where each point is in the right order; one flows onto the next, onto the next, and onto the next.

Too often I see people have them in the wrong order, and it comes out as a segmented talk with different points and overarching messages throughout, with no clear connection. Most of the time, this happens when people try to over-teach.

It's important to reverse engineer your presentation.

Be clear on your overarching message and ensure it is going to resonate with your audience. Now you can figure out how your points are going to serve your message and interlink. Doing this allows you to never have to say in a talk again, "and for my next point", which makes me die a little inside every time I hear it.

Do this right, and it seamlessly leads to your conclusion, aka, the call to action. Your call to action is what you want the audience to go out and do, to consider, to sign up for, to join.

This isn't saying "in conclusion" and recapping what you said. This is leaving people with one clear task on what they need to do. Make them leave knowing clearly what the next step is. Sign a contract with your company, join your future based movement, cherish your loved ones, live a healthier life, or whatever your message might be.

You can now apply this blueprint to every talk you ever give. Knowing this alone will allow you to put in 20% of the effort you have in the past, and be better than 80% of other speakers out there.

Chapter 9: Getting your Facts Right

Before you get ready for public speaking, always ensure that you have your facts right. There are some important things that you need to know about in as far as fact finding is concerned. The following are the important things that you have to remember at all times:

How long you are going to be speaking

This is the first thing that you need to know about when preparing for a public speech. The length of time you will spend speaking is important so you can plan ahead. You may come prepared for a 20 minute speech, only to get shocked when you are supposed to deliver an hour's worth of speeches. This will definitely set you back, and can also interfere with your

thought process.

Know the audience

Public speech is all about understanding your audience. You have to know beforehand the composition of the audience. It is important to know how many of the support your idea and which ones do not support the idea. There are audiences that can be predetermined early enough, especially in the event that you are about to deliver a speech on a contentious issue.

The time of the speech

It is always a good idea to try and know beforehand the time of the day wherein you will be giving the speech. The importance of knowing the time is because it helps you plan ahead of time not only for the speech you are about to deliver, but to help you anticipate the mood that your audience will be in. This is because naturally, people can be in different moods in the morning as compared to their moods in the evenings.

The nature of the speech program

Understand what the rest of the speech program is all about. This is important to help you decipher how receptive the audience will be when you are giving your speech. It helps to know beforehand whether you are going to be the first, fifth or last speaker, so that you can come prepared to deal with the emotions of the audience after the other speakers have done their thing.

It also helps to know who the other speakers are, because if you are making a speech after President Obama has made his, chances are high that you will really need to be on top of your game. Actually, you will need a miracle to keep the audience in the same emotion as he has, or to sustain their level of anticipation based on the speech that they have just been exposed to.

Getting the answers to these questions will help you determine how to plan your speech, and most importantly how to deliver it in the best way possible.

The bottom line about public speaking is the fact that when you are delivering a speech, you will be delivering the speech to someone, and about something. It is therefore important to know who these people are and what the subject means.

The following are some questions that you will need to ask before you go on to deliver a speech, so that you can plan properly for the same.

What is the name of the event, the time, venue and date?

What topic are you supposed to address?

How long is the speech supposed to last?

What is the main agenda that the speech is supposed to achieve?

Is it possible to get access to the main agenda of the speech?

Who will introduce you, and is it possible if you can send them a prepared introductory note?

Who do you refer to in the event that you need more information?

If possible, get to know about the useful demographics about the audience. The following are some of the important things that you need to know about your audience.

How many people will be in the audience? The demographics about the audience (the age, occupation, gender, background) – at this point, try to know anything possible that can help you make a difference

What is their attitude towards the topic?

Will the audience be allowed to ask questions during the speech or after?

Will you be allowed to mingle with and socialize with the audience before, during or after the speech is over?

The answers to these questions will go so far in ensuring that you are able to deliver a really good speech, one that the audience will remember for a very long time.

Chapter 10: Prepare, Prepare, Prepare.

As you go about observing other public speakers to learn their tricks, one thing that stands out is something that we all want when we must give a talk to a group.

That thing is confidence. Confidence is not something you cannot buy in a can and it doesn't come automatically. But it is a quality in a public speaker that puts an audience at ease and makes it much easier to get your message across.

There are plenty of tricks of the trade for improving your confidence as you prepare for that public speaking moment. Like anything else, experienced public speakers know these tricks and use them extensively. There is one word that summarized the number one way to get your confidence up and that word is preparation. When that seasoned public speaker walks confidently to the podium, he or she is confident because of preparation. There are three kinds of preparation that you can do that will vastly improve your confidence when it is your turn to wow that crowd with your presentation.

Preparation Through Experience.

As is true in anything, experience is what makes all of the difference between a nervous novice public speaker and a seasoned old pro. The problem with experience is that if you don't have any, it isn't easy to get. But there are ways you can increase your body of experience before a major presentation so at least you get in the flow of how to stand in front of a group of people and talk.

There are groups that specialize in making you a better public speaker. Of course, you can take a course in public speaking at the local learning outlet or Junior College and that will help you learn in a formal way how to organize and present a speech and it will give you the exposure to actually speaking to groups through in class experiences. There are other groups like the Toastmasters that also can help you become a better speaker.

Above all, look for chances to speak to groups. It might be giving a toast at a wedding, offering to read to children at the local library or teaching Sunday School at church. By exposing yourself to public speaking situations, you can gain that much needed experience in public speaking that will give you the confidence of an old pro.

Preparation Through Research

Confidence also comes because you know that what you are presenting is well researched and that it will stand up to scrutiny. The research phase of your preparation happens as you write your speech.

Be sure you take the time to read up on your topic and become an expert in what you are speaking about. By exposing yourself to what others have to say, you will become both knowledgeable about your topic and passionate about the position you are going to discuss. Being knowledgeable and passionate about your topic are the very essence of confidence and those qualities can put your topic over the top in helping those listening agree with you and feel a desire to go along with your recommendations.

Preparation Through Knowledge.

Many times when a public speaker gets up to talk and those butterflies begin to fly around in the stomach, they wonder why this happens. What is often not recognized is that you are feeling insecure that something might happen that will cause you to not deliver your material correctly. Much of that insecurity comes from not knowing your material extraordinarily well and you know deep down that it not be hard for you to get distracted or disoriented when speaking to a crowd.

We are not going to lie to you, those distractions happen. One way to vanquish that feeling that you are not sure about your material is to know your presentation inside and out. If you know every point of that outline, every illustration and every transition so well that you can literally give that talk in your sleep, the chances you will flounder in front of a crowd all but vanish.

There is no magic to getting to this level of knowledge. Knowledge of your talk only comes through hard work. Write your talk yourself because then it will be in your own words and you will understand everything in it from day one. Reach and review the text and the outline of your presentation until you can see those notes in front of your eyes in the dark. Practice giving your talk and review it often even up to moments before you get up to speak.

This is knowledge that is beyond memorization. You should know that presentation with the same familiarity that you know the names of your family and your personal history. It should flow out of you easily and naturally. Actors know this trick and experienced performers stand up with that script so well in mind that they virtually could have written it themselves. Get to that point with your presentation and you will walk to that podium with that confidence that you know your stuff, you believe in it and you are ready to tell the world what you have to say.

Chapter 11: How Do I Prepare For An Impromptu Talk?

Wow. This is a tough one. It's like preparing for a spontaneous vacation. This is where it's crucial that you know your content. You must know the problem and how it can be fixed, and the steps to get there. You must be able to talk this stuff backwards and forwards. I do a lot of speech memorization and practicing in the car while I'm driving. Sometimes I will just practice reciting the content and explaining it in a way that makes sense and gets right to the point. And I make sure they aren't just scripted words, but words I really believe in. They aren't my scripts, they're my truths.

Blogging really helps me in this area too. I end up talking about my content over and over and over and over. Eventually I just know it.

Being able to talk your talk will come in handy when you sell your speeches too.

This is the sales talk you will use with your clients when they want to know what you speak about. This is also the wording you will put on your website – the strongest place you have to sell yourself other than them seeing you speak.

There is one case that I can think of right now where the talk is truly impromptu in nature - beauty pageants. Not that I was ever in one. But I think their questions are a surprise for the contestants. And maybe you are asked at the last minute to step in for someone and speak. Or maybe you're in a meeting and you've been asked to get up and speak. If you truly don't have time to prepare your content ahead of time, then here is what I can suggest to help you prepare for what you can't prepare for.

Relax. If you wig out, you'll perform poorly.   Breathe.

Listen before you start. Take a moment to think before you start. If you can. Don't try to be a polished speaker with a great answer. Don't try to use stunning language or be somebody you're not. Just answer the question. Address the issue. Say the words, "I believe..." and then go. Don't be afraid to ask questions (if you can). Sometimes we think that standing at the podium means we aren't allowed to talk to the audience. Not true. If you need to ask Jim in the front row a question (I'm assuming it's on topic) then go ahead. Resist the urge to talk too much. This is the biggest issue when people don't prepare. They ramble. They repeat points, or even beat them to death. Be brief. Nobody ever minds a speaker who goes short.

PS To all you beauty pageant contestants out there who might get stuck with a question they simply don't have the answer to: I would probably say something like, "I have never really given that question any thought. Which is exactly what is wrong with the world today. We go through the motions and never look up to see what's important." Doesn't hurt to make a joke. Funny always warms up an audience and relieves the tension. As long as it's clean, let it rip. (If you're not funny, then you need to find the book in this series on learning to be funny.)

Should I Personalize My Presentation?

Yes! Yes! Yes! And Yes! People are impacted by people they believe, like, know, and trust. If you want to influence them, you need for them to feel like they know you – not the polished version of you – but the real you.

How do you do this? Admit some of the quirky things about yourself. Admit your weaknesses. Talk about mistakes you've made and how you've learned from them. What you did right will not affect them as much as what you did wrong.

In my career as a motivational speaker, I was surprised to find that it's not my perfection that people connect to, but rather my imperfection. People connect to those they can relate to, and most people in an audience don't feel perfect.

Chapter 12: Make sure to move...

We're now going to talk about the physical components of the presentation. You've done a great job with the verbal components. Nothing you are going to say will detract from the message you are trying to convey.

Now, let's make sure that nothing you physically do will detract from your presentation's message as well.

A great way to detract from your presentation is to look extremely unnatural. This could mean:

Standing perfectly straight and not moving

Staring at note cards

Not making eye contact with anyone

We're going to talk about how to avoid each one of these components, so you look completely natural. Let's begin with the perfectly straight, not moving example.

Standing perfectly straight

This always catches the audience's eye. In your day to day life, you are never perfectly straight in any facet of life. If you are perfectly straight and not moving during your presentation, it will look weird. You will come across as stiff, unnatural, and tense. Not the message you want to communicate to your audience!

Standing perfectly straight exercise: the planned move

Fortunately, there is an incredibly easy fix here. We're looking for the "planned move" across the stage.

Assuming you are standing up for this presentation, you'll probably have a fair amount of space. You could be on a stage, standing in front of a screen, or perhaps behind a podium.

The trick is to find a place within your prepared remarks to move. This will automatically loosen you up and will create a more natural look to the presentation.

A standard "move" opportunity I've coached my students is a transition from problem to solution. A lot of speeches in corporate settings involve highlighting a problem, then describing a solution.

Let's assume you are standing by a projector screen. Start on one side of the screen as you talk through the problem. Then, walk to the other side of the screen as you say: "I just highlighted (the problem). Now, let's talk about the solution."

This will not only look more natural, but it also creates a physical differentiation in your presentation for different topics. It's a small tip, but it works quite well.

Staring at note cards

Another common issue. Many presenters love bringing note cards with them to reference during a presentation. The issue is note cards create a logical place for you to stare during the presentation. You glance down for a second, then suddenly you're staring at them the whole time.

Even worse, note cards make you look unprepared or unprofessional to your audience.

Start at note cards exercise: NO!

Here's the simple solution: never use notecards again. I outlaw all of my students from using note cards in a presentation. If you take one thing away from this book, it's never to use notecards again.

It's so simple to get rid of them. They're small anyway, so you can't fit much on them anyways. You could quickly memorize what is on the notecards. Just ignore the notecards!

Not making eye contact

We just threw out your notecards, so we have eliminated one thing you could have looked at during your presentation. Now, we're going to make sure you make eye contact.

The lack of eye contact is a great way to make your audience disengaged with your presentation. By making eye contact, you will draw your audience into the presentation and make them feel like they are a part of what you are saying.

Unfortunately, this frequently goes wrong. Many people either don't make eye contact at all (staring at the ground) or try to make eye contact with an entire audience of hundreds (look like a bobblehead).

Not making eye contact exercise: pick three people

This exercise is straightforward. When you give your presentation, pick out three people in the audience to make eye contact with. One on your left, one straight in front of you, and one to your right.

When speaking, simply make eye contact with those three people. Shift your gaze between each of them, and you'll cover the entire spectrum of the audience. The entire audience will feel engaged, and all you were really doing is making eye contact with only three people.

Chapter 13: PREPARATION IS (USUALLY) THE KEY!

As mentioned from the previous chapters, preparation is important when it comes to public speaking. Constant practice and preparing for your speech is important as it helps you in knowing the content of your topic while at the same time making you feel at ease while talking with the crowd. In order to fully prepare for your upcoming challenge you need to learn a couple of important steps.

The first step when it comes to preparing for a speech is to learn your topic. Again, you need to research your subject and you need to be as concise as possible. Never waste the time of your listeners. Learn how to get straight to the point and remember to focus only on the topic at hand. Never get side tracked or use a reference which is unknown to you. For instance, you should never use a quote from an unknown source. If you want to use a quote then you should make sure you know who said it and what the context was.

The next step in preparing for your speech is your presentation. Presentation is also important when it comes to public speaking since most people tend to judge a person through what they see and not on what they hear. Therefore, you need to prepare some visual aids. Chapter 6 focuses on the tools that we often use when we are speaking with the public. Along with those tools, you also need to focus on your appearance. Taking care of your appearance will not only make you feel more confident but it will also make you look professional to the crowd.

The next step is on venue preparation. The environment where you will perform is very important. If you have access to the venue then you can rehearse before your show. Preparing your visual aids before your big speech is definitely important. However, if you have the opportunity to become familiar with your venue, you should take advantage of it.

Finally, you need to practice. Practice makes perfect. You need to practice in front of a mirror or in front of your family and friends before your big day. Learn to study your speech and follow proper pacing. If you will be applying any body movements then you need to make them as natural as possible.

However, too much preparation is also not prescribed. The reason for this is that if you prepare too much on your speech, it will often seem too mechanical and too rehearsed. Your audience will see that your speech is not natural and they might tune you out. Therefore, you need to understand that there is a small margin for error when it comes to preparing effectively and over preparation. Focus on making your speech appear natural and unrehearsed.

Chapter 14: Never Practice In Front of The Mirror

Can you observe the speed of the train if you are inside the train? NO, to observe you have to be outside. Can you observe the speed of the flight if you are inside the flight? No, to observe that speed you have to be outside the flight. If you are a part of the process, you cannot observe the process it is very difficult.

When we practice in front of the mirror we are trying to do the same thing. We are involved in the process and at the same time we are trying to observe the process, which is not possible, it is extremely difficult.

That's why it's very important that there has to be someone else observing you. Mirror can't give you feedback.

But most of the time that someone else who can observe

you from the outside is not available. Maybe your friend your colleagues maybe someone else who can observe you they are not there to help you.

But there is something which is available most of the times and maybe that something is in your hand right now your smart phone.

Yes, next time when you have any presentation, or talk, or

speech, instead of practicing in front of the mirror practice in front of the camera.

Record your session and then there are three ways in which you can observe your video recording

1. Mute it and just observe your body language. You know

55 % your body language contributes towards effective communication

2. Just listen to it. Observe your vocal variety. You know

38% vocal variety contributes towards effective communication

3. And lastly observe everything together

Now when you are observing you are not a part of the process. You are observing it from outside. Make notes and next time when you are doing a rehearsal or practicing the session again try to implement these observations which you have observed as an outsider.

So for your next presentation OR next speech OR next talk stop practicing in front of the mirror and start practicing in front of the camera.

8. How Not to End a Presentation

So how much time do I have? Is my time over? I think I'm running out of time. How many times you have seen people closing the presentation like this. Closing your presentation like this is one of the weakest ways to close your presentations.

According to experts, the last part of your presentation, last few lines, the last few words are the most important, why? Because last words linger in the minds of the audience.

But if you are closing like this, it's a very weak ending. So how to avoid closing like "how much time do we have", the easiest way is to use a stopwatch, not the watch but a stopwatch. Now if you are relying on the watch, imagine for a moment that you have a presentation from 2:00 to 3:00

you have started your presentation. Now in the middle of the talk, you want to see how much more time you have? you look at your watch and then you go back on your memory lane and ask yourself whether you have started at 2:00 or

2.10 or maybe early maybe late. It is difficult to calculate time in the middle of the presentation and you are never confirmed about it. You're never 100% sure about it.

But if you use a stopwatch, it can help. Just before you go

for the presentation maybe, 5 minutes before jus,t start the stopwatch. Do not wait for the last moment to start your stopwatch.

Now at any point in time, you have complete awareness of the time. You know how much time you have spent, how much time you have.

And remember the audience always respect those speakers who respect time. So next time when you are going on the stage make sure you use a stopwatch. So you don't have to close your presentation like "how much time I have?" and if you're not going on the stage, start going because if you want to be a leader in your life you have to separate yourself from the crowd, stand alone and speak.

CHAPTER 15: PUTTING YOUR PRESENTATION TOGETHER

Mark Twain said, "It usually takes me two or three days to prepare an impromptu speech." The more prepared you are, the less anxiety you will experience when you make your presentation, regardless of the length of the presentation. In fact, while preparing your presentation, you may start to change your view of public speaking. You might start to get somewhat excited to share this information or heart-felt message with others. There are several pieces to it and you should approach the preparation in the order I have created for you.

KNOW YOUR AUDIENCE

When you set your expectations, knowing your audience will have a great impact on your success. All audiences appreciate that you are familiar with them in one way or another. Connecting with them will make you one of them and remind them that you're human.

If you are speaking to a group of people in the same industry in which you work, you will have a great opportunity to create material that will evoke laughter based on those idiosyncrasies associated with your industry. Acronyms, environment, clientele. Just a handful of similarities that you will have. However, always keep this in mind; humor should always be appropriate and respectful. You might want to run your material by a trusted colleague to make sure it is appropriate.

If you are speaking to a group in your community, you should do your homework to make sure you understand the subjects that evoke a positive feeling and those subjects that tend to be taboo and/or are politically incorrect. If you have an opportunity to attend a gathering of this group before you do your presentation, you'll have a better feel for what they're looking for. And, of course, the Internet can give you a lot of information on any local group.

When you have been invited to speak to an audience at a school, the most obvious tip is to understand age-appropriate material. Never talk down to your audience. Your priority is to lift them up.

I was invited to teach a group of High School Seniors assertive communication skills. I had three separate sessions with them. The first session was designed to teach them the skills and how to use them in real-life scenarios. In following weeks, we had two additional sessions where they shared their experiences in those real-life scenarios.

The most important part of the first session was to make sure they understood the difference between assertive and aggressive communication. And, most importantly, the benefit to them for being more assertive rather than aggressive. This session was a 3-hour workshop with one or two breaks built in to keep them engaged.

I treated them the same way I would treat adults in a professional environment attending the same type of workshop. There was a young man in the audience who was wearing his baseball cap backwards. He was slumped down in his chair and trying to look completely uninterested and, probably for his age-group, very cool.

I started by explaining how our day would progress. I told them I appreciated that this information is not normally something high-school students had an opportunity to learn and that, in fact, many adults in the work environment never had the opportunity either. I let them know that the skills I would introduce to them to would help them positively influence others in many situations. My plan, I told them, was to treat them with respect and I would appreciate it if they could be respectful, as well. When I said that last part, I made direct eye contact with that young man. I paused for effect. I did not say another word. I continued to look right at him. He got the message. He sat up and took off his baseball cap. Then I continued, and these young men and women learned very valuable skills.

At the end of the first day, he waited until almost everybody had left. He walked up to me, extended his hand, and thanked me for having an impact on him. Now, that's a rewarding day!

The success there is that, in knowing my audience, I was able to create a workshop that would impact them for the rest of their lives.

My primary audience tends to be Managers/Leaders in the private and public sector. The one connection I realize I always have with them is understanding what their real day at work most likely looks like. I've learned that basically the work environment is a place comprised of men and women with different personalities, from different generations and different life experiences, who are thrown together for a certain number of hours over a certain number of days and expected to produce results. You can change the type of work environment: office, hospital, government building, non-profit, manufacturing plant, farm, ranch, or retail store (If I left yours out, I apologize). What I tend to focus on is how people, thrown together, can get results by working better together.

Who is your audience? It's the first part of creating your presentation. Know who you're presenting to.

CHOOSE YOUR SUBJECT

This sounds somewhat obvious, right? I was once assigned a workshop on How to Organize Files and Records. This was supposed to be a 6-hour workshop. I had no actual working knowledge of how to do this. I was even given an outline for the presentation and a plethora of resource information. It was my job to create content to fill the entire 6-HOUR WORKSHOP. As experienced as I am as a Professional Speaker, I failed miserably. I felt like most of the content was just fluff to get through the workshop. I think I may have actually tap-danced for a small portion of that workshop. That was the last time I let somebody else give me an assignment where I simply did not have enough knowledge to give a credible presentation.

Though people tell me they are terrified of public speaking, most all of them admit that they are much more comfortable if they are talking about a subject in which they have a high level of knowledge. That's because you know what you know.

Don't be afraid, however, to step out of your comfort zone and learn something new to teach others. When I teach workshops, I ask the participants to learn as if they will need to teach the skills they are learning to others. Try this the next time a new skill, process, or procedure is being taught to you. You will be amazed at how much more you will retain when you believe you have to teach it to others.

I have spent a great deal of my adult life in the banking industry. In banking, we have changes in policies and procedures all the time. I don't have time to attend every class or conference call regarding these changes. I'll ask one of my employees to attend the class or call in my stead. Then they are to share the information to the entire staff at our weekly meeting. They always comment on how they pay more attention to the learning process when they are the teacher.

In Chapter 6, we will take your subject and I'll help you put it together in a way that will work for you and your audience.

You're probably wondering why I put "Know Your Audience" before "Choose Your Subject." You could choose which subject you'd like to speak about, but it may not be appropriate or relevant to your audience. Knowing your audience and their expectations will help you create a presentation they will appreciate.

PROPS:

Now that you know your audience, and you've chosen your subject, you will need to decide how you want to present your material. So many options are available. It's also a delicate balance. This is where many nervous people opt to have a visual aid that will take the focus off of them. Depending on the subject matter, a visual aid could be a "must" or a "bust." You also need to take into account your audience. Sixth-graders might not be terribly impressed with your PowerPoint presentation (they can probably already build a more impressive one). But they would love it if you tossed a few giveaways (related to your topic) into the audience to change things up. On the other hand, co-workers, employees, and all-adult attendees wouldn't mind getting a little sweet treat for participating. So,

117

remember to tie your props to your audience and subject matter.

Let's look at our options for props:

PowerPoint Presentations: This can be tricky. You must, must, must make sure you have practiced several times, at home, before ever doing one of these presentations in front of your audience. Always get to the venue a bit early and make sure you have all necessary cords and they are connected correctly. Check the volume control for the flat screen. Make sure you know where the light switches are. It's not a good idea to turn the lights completely off. Your audience might be of the note-taking persuasion. You should, however, be able to dim the lights so the presentation is easily seen by the audience. When you have a mishap with any technology, you will experience increased anxiety, lose focus, and will not have the desired result you were anticipating. Always make hard copies of your PowerPoint presentation, just in case of a mishap. Or, get the email address for all participants and send them the PowerPoint presentation.

Prezi: This is a fantastic cloud-based program that can be referred to as "PowerPoint on steroids." You start with a virtual canvas and create a story for your audience. It's very easy to learn. You can use templates that are already created for you. You simply write the story. Or you can use a blank canvas. You can even take an already created PowerPoint presentation and insert it onto a canvas. You can insert music, videos, and pictures. Look it up online. I'm confident you'll love it!

Flip Charts: Old school and still reliable. Flip charts are not high-tech, and that is exactly why audiences still enjoy them. Creating your visual in front of your audience is a way of keeping their attention throughout the presentation.

Flip charts are great when you plan to do a presentation where your audience will be creatively participating. Set them up around the room, hand out some colored markers, and cut them loose! If you use flip charts in a group exercise, you still want to make sure they are stable when you set them up. Also, placing them around the room so small groups can converse and create is very important. Setting them up too close to one another can create a noise issue that will distract from the creativity you were hoping for. Give very specific timeframes for completion of a group activity and stick with it.

Handouts: We've all gotten these at a presentation. Some we use and some we don't. Handouts should be something you want your audience to take with them. The information should be of value and something they will refer to long after they've seen your presentation. I attended a quarterly meeting where one department gave us a handout with photos of the people representing that department. Quite frankly, this handout had little use as I already had their contact information in the signature of their email.

Make sure all of your contact information is on the handout, if you choose to have one. Invite participants to contact you with any follow-up questions they might have. If you have everybody's contact information at your disposal, answer their question and send it out to all participants. Many people have the same questions after a presentation...only the brave will ask them.

Depending on the length of your presentation, your handout could be a workbook. I still have workbooks from seminars I attended 20 years ago. A lot of information is timeless and still relates to situations I encounter in everyday life.

Chapter 16: How To Use Stories And Quotations In Your Speech

Learning how to use stories and quotations in your speech is useful in many situations. Bringing a topic or point to life is important if you want to grab the listener's attention and get the message across. Stories are a great way of doing this. There are many ways in which you can bring the real-life aspect into a speech, making it more effective.

It is helpful to have something stored at the back of your mind in case you feel you need to change the pace of the presentation. Often you won't know who the audience is and the way you tell your stories are important. You would use a different tone with a group of businessmen than you would for a couple of teenagers. Here, you have to be spontaneous.

If you want to really emphasize a point, a story is going to help do the job. However, you have to think about this, before you unleash. Something like this has to be relevant. This may sound obvious, but some people just go overboard, often thinking out loud. In a case like this, the story is going to do more harm than good.

If you are feeling nervous or you feel that you need to capture the audience from the start, then break into a humorous story in the beginning. This often works well for school kids, who you may find are more difficult to get the full attention of. Sometimes, laughing at yourself can do a lot for the rest of the speech.

Some people are natural story tellers and are able to make up something from nothing, but some people are not so lucky. It just requires more thought and planning to be able to pull something off. Skip the details and focus on the essentials, making it unique.

Keep them short and sweet as well. A lot of people drift off if they have to concentrate on one aspect for too long. A story is more effective if it is shortened, where the listener is able to find the punch line easier. Often this is just lost with anything that is lengthy.

In the case of quotations, you will find it helpful to draw parallels between the life of a famous speaker, and a topic that relates to the speech. Be careful of adding humorous quotes. Make sure you use them at the right time. It is also important to use quotes appropriately, depending on your audience. You may have to stick to basic humor for a certain age group, but you will probably have to change it around in another situation.

Once you have learned how to use stories and quotations in your speech, you will start to see a big difference in the way you can capture the audience. It takes some effort to get a particular message across and you have to make use of all of your resources. This may not be simple in the beginning if you are not a natural story teller, but the more you practice, the easier it will get.

Chapter 17: BUILD YOUR CONFIDENCE

Nobody is born with limitless self-confidence. If someone seems to have incredible self-confidence, it's because he or she has worked on building it for years. Self-confidence is something that you learn to build up because the challenging world of business and life in general, can deflate it.

Here are some things you can do to build up your self-confidence as a Speaker.

Identify Yourself and Find Your Source of Shyness

Each person experiences his or her shyness in a unique way or identity, so you have to, first of all, identify yourself and understand what situations trigger this feeling of fear or shyness and why? For example, do you have stomach pains when you are asked to speak in public or do you feel shy or nervous when speaking to a large group of people for the first time? When you are able to identify yourself and understand yourself and your source of shyness, you can now begin to overcome your shyness by examining the nature of your fear or shyness and practicing to overcome it.

Start With Very, Very Small Talk and Simple Actions:

Get your feet wet. Shy people often report that they have trouble talking with people they have just met, particularly those people to whom they might feel attracted. A strategy for helping shy people to overcome this inhibition is to start with relatively non-threatening situations and very small talk. Non-threatening situations might include malls, museums, political rallies, or sporting events where you will have the opportunity to interact with a lot of people for a relatively brief period of time. In such interactions, you can start by smiling and saying something simple like "hello" to as many people as you care to make eye contact with and who will smile at you. Asking for simple directions, giving an unexpected compliment, or offering assistance (e.g., offer to hold a door) are three very simple ways to practice talking with people. Thus, the point here is to get used to talking with others.

Develop Conversation Skills: How To Keep Talking.

Shy people who have mastered the art of small talk can take the next step by developing their conversational skills. The trick to a successful conversation is to have something to say. There are a number of very simple strategies that shy people can employ to make sure they have something to say. You can start by reading the newspaper or magazines and/or listening to information-based radio programs. The advantage of such information sources is that they also give you the type of in-depth, "behind-the-headlines" analysis that is the basic substance of much social conversation. Shy people can also do their part to help keep the conversation going by asking open-ended questions that require more than a yes or no answer (e.g., What do you think of . . . ?).

Come To Terms with Audience Expressions

Your anxiety level is increased when you misinterpret the audience's facial expression. In normal conversation, we're accustomed to getting feedback from the listener—a nod or a smile here and there that signal approval. But when we present, audiences listen differently. They're more likely to give the speaker a blank stare, which doesn't mean they don't like what they hear; more often than not, it simply means they're concentrating on the message. This is especially true of audience members who are introverted.

Become an Expert on Your Topic

You will greatly increase your confidence and success as a public speaker by thoroughly researching your topic. What you present in your speech comprises only a small portion of what you know about the topic. If you don't do your research, you will be nervous about your speech.

Learn To Take Rejection: No One Is Liked By Everyone.

Rejection is one of the risks that accompany engaging in social interactions. A key to overcoming shyness is not to take rejection personally. There may be a variety of reasons that someone is rejected by someone else, none of which may have anything at all to do with the person being rejected. For example, one person may not like what the shy person is wearing, and another person may be bored with the entire social situation, not just with her conversation with the shy individual. The point is that sometimes you can control the reactions of others (e.g., by wearing stylish clothes) and at other times you cannot. What's important is that shy people make a realistic attempt to socialize with others.

Find Your Comfort Zone: Do What Fits You.

Not all social situations are for everyone. For example, some shy people might be uneasy in a bar or nightclub where physical attractiveness and stylish dress are critical predictors of social success. In other situations, extensive knowledge of politics, art, or murder mysteries might be the key to success. Shy people should seek out those situations that are most consistent with their temperament and interests. It is easier for shy people to overcome or manage their sense of social anxiety and self-consciousness by finding situations in which they feel reasonably comfortable. Volunteering for different organizations is a good strategy for shy people to use in an attempt to find various places where they might feel comfortable. In most cases, being a volunteer requires a low level of skills, offers the possibility of meeting many different types of people, and is easy to terminate if the experience does not turn out to be what was expected. Thus, overcoming shyness can be helped by seeking out an assortment of volunteer experiences as a means of meeting new people, practicing social skills in different situations, and helping to find those social situations that are the most comfortable

Practice As If You're the Worst

When you know your material well, there's a tendency to get sloppy when practicing a speech: You might flip through the slides, mentally thinking about what you are going to say, without actually rehearsing out loud exactly what you plan to say. This results in a presentation that's not as sharp as it could be and might cause you to be nervous once you have 100 pairs of eyes staring at you.

Focus on Your Message, Not on Your Fear

The more you think about being anxious about speaking, the more you will increase your level of anxiety. Instead, in the few minutes before you speak, mentally review your major ideas, your introduction, and your conclusion. Focus on your ideas rather than on your fear.

Visualize Your Success

Imagine yourself giving your speech. Picture yourself walking confidently to the front and delivering your well prepared opening remarks. Visualize yourself giving the entire speech as a controlled, confident speaker. Imagine yourself calm and in command.

Practice Breathing Exercises

Proper breathing technique is fundamental to having a strong, confident speaking voice. Performing some simple exercises will help you to project your sound and maintain a relaxed manner while speaking. Breathing exercises are particularly useful when you are preparing to speak in front of a group.

Posture

In order to breathe properly, you must stand in a posture that facilitates deep inhalation and exhalation. Stand with your feet nearly shoulder-width apart, distributing your weight on both balls of your feet and your heels. With each exhalation, release tension in your shoulders and relax your neck and jaws.

Exaggerated Movement Exercise

A relaxed jaw and throat facilitate deep breathing. Rosemary Scott Vohs, storytelling and speech communication instructor at Western Washington University, suggests making some exaggerated movements with your face to ease tension in the jaw and open the throat. First, lift the eyebrows and open the mouth wide. Then, yawn widely and loudly, saying "yah, yah, yah." Stretch your mouth, saying "eee, ooo, eee, ooo," in an exaggerated fashion.

Know Your Introduction and Conclusion Well

Successfully presenting the introduction of your speech will boost your confidence, help calm your nerves, and reduce worrisome thoughts that increase anxiety. Knowing that you'll finish with a coherent, smooth, and memorable conclusion will increase your confidence and lessen your nervousness throughout your speech. One useful strategy for knowing your introduction and conclusion well is to write them out word for word. Then read them aloud a few times, listening to how they sound and making any necessary changes. Once you're satisfied with your introduction and conclusion, commit them to memory as best you can. Although generally, you don't want to memorize your entire speech, memorizing your introduction and conclusion will help you present them more fluently and lessen your anxiety.

Chapter 18: Getting and Developing Ideas

What are you curious about? It's often been said that one of the best ways to learn about something is to research the topic and then give a speech about it. Maybe there's something you always wondered about or wanted to learn more about. Why not research it and make it the basis of your next speech. Often ideas can come from our own lives. How has something in our pasts affected us? How do we feel about it? Can others identify with our feelings, and is it likely they've been in similar circumstances? Do my feeling have importance to others?

As a young boy, a Southern California man was sent to a German concentration camp during World War II. Only he and his sister survived the ordeal. His brother was tortured to death, and his parents starved. After the war the man came to the U.S. where he worked as a chef. Later he published a book about his experiences and then began a second career talking about his early life.

Though few in his audiences had similar experiences, they could certainly relate to his feelings.

Another consideration when looking for a topic is that almost anything can present us with ideas for a speech. Seeing a person abusing an animal can lead us to talk about the subject overall. Seeing homeless people can convince us to do research and talk about the problems of homelessness.

Ideas also can come from things we read that inspire us—a person overcoming major problems, for instance. Or something we read or see on television can make us angry enough to want to change the situation. Examples might be bullying on the job, or government waste. Examine how you feel about a subject and why you feel that way. Figure out what you can do about it.

Examine your beliefs. What is important to you? Why? Do others feel as you do about the same subject? If so, share your experiences with the audience. If not, give a talk in which you try to change their minds.

Getting Ideas

I was walking down the street, glancing out across the sunlit Pacific, dreaming of the fame and riches my public speaking career would bring. Suddenly, a man in a shabby suit coat and torn jeans rushed up and blocked my path.

"Excuse me," I said as I tried to step around him. He was the one who should have yielded, of course, but I was in a mellow mood.

Again, he leaped in front of me. "Have I got a deal for you!" he said, his voice as raspy as an old bass fiddle. I expected him to fling open his coat to show me a row of cheap watches pinned inside. Instead, he thrust out his hand, and I saw that he clutched a dozen glass tubes, each a foot long and transparent.

He must have seen my puzzled expression. "They're ideas," he said. "Elusive, hard to pin down. But captured here forever in glass...or at least till you break them open and use them."

He edged closer and peered intently into my eyes. "How about it?" he asked. "Only a dime a dozen!"

Ideas for giving speeches really are a dime a dozen. Suppose you are going to give a talk on whatever topic you choose. How do you come up with ideas—besides, of course, examining your own interests and background? Well, ahead of time, you should determine as much as you can about the sort of audience you'll have. The more you know about your listeners, the better you can direct your speech to them. For instance, are they a group of high school student or college students? Or are they senior citizens or members of a social group?

Suppose you're a biologist talking to a group of biologists. The speech you give there would be vastly different than would a talk on the same subject to a group of laymen or to a group of middle school kids.

This, on a smaller scale, of course, is what television network does in determining potential audiences for a series. The more you know about an audience, the better a speech you can give, a speech that appeals to them or is of interest, no matter what the reason.

Why Are You Giving This Talk?

You've been chosen to give a speech. First, why you? Is it because you're an expert? Do you know a lot more about the subject than most other people? If so, that's a good reason it's you who will give the talk. Or maybe you just have a strong interest in the subject and would like to share this interest with others. Maybe you're going to talk to members of a particular interest group. Say you belong to a bird-watching society and have fallen in love with a particular type of bird. You're so enthusiastic about it that you want to interest others too.

Maybe you're so fired up about something that you would do anything you could to defend it or maybe to get rid of it—like a certain ballot measure. Whatever the subject and whatever the reason, you need to put a lot of thought into it. For one thing you have to decide on your approach. This involves a central idea: the main point of the speech. Examples could be: "Animal abuse laws need to be strengthened." So you've chosen animal abuse as the general topic and have narrowed it to laws about animal abuse. You've also chosen the angle or approach. You want to convince the audience that there needed to be stricter rules for those who abuse animals.

Even if you're an expert or are very knowledgeable about a subject, your preparation should include investigating the subject further. Maybe there's something that can help with your talk that you've overlooked. Maybe someone else has found an aspect you've not considered or even known about; maybe you find something that could poke a big hole in what you want to say. It's certainly better to find this out beforehand.

No matter what, try to be as well-prepared as possible, and be prepared to adjust to the audience as well as you can, or the results can be less than desirable. For instance, a few years ago a man was asked to give a talk about publishing, not only in a foreign country, but where he knew only the person who'd asked him to give the talk. The problem was the man who asked him to speak didn't tell much ahead of time about the audience, so he assumed certain things that turned out to be very wrong. He was told he was to be the keynote speaker. But what he didn't know was that there was to be entertainment following his speech, entertainment that consisted of several different parts.

The speaker had prepared a ten-minute talk, semi-serious, but with a lot of humor thrown in. And the speaker was no novice. Yet about two minutes into his talk he found that no one was paying attention. People were shuffling their feet, whispering to each other, coughing, and doing a lot of shifting in their chairs. Since he was an experienced speaker, this was an unusual reaction, which affected him so much that his mouth became dry and he had trouble speaking. He cut the speech very short, and red-faced, went back to his chair.

The point of this is that you should determine all you can about the audience and the event. The speaker was under the impression that he was "the main event" when, in effect, he shouldn't have given the talk at all because the only thing the audience cared about was the upcoming entertainment. The problem could have been avoided by asking questions about the event, about the evening's program, and about the audience.

Chapter 19: Afterglow

This feeling carried on the following week at work. On Monday the head of my department congratulated me personally for "a great speech", as did the Chief Financial Officer when I bumped into him in the lift. Working for one of the largest companies in Europe, this was quite something. Neither had seen it themselves but word had spread in this small city. The CFO told me his wife and daughter had been in the audience and said my talk was the best of the day. The mutual back-patting continued online over the following days between the speakers and event organisers.

A former boss and good friend of mine, Marty Hirsch, told me that even his hairdresser had commented about my talk to him: "He said you were just what the audience needed at the time you came on. Apparently, there had been a bit of a lull. He said you were charismatic, hilarious, spot on, and brilliant! He said you had the capacity crowd in your hand."

Once the euphoria of the TEDx event had subsided, along came the excitement of seeing our talks online, on the official TEDx YouTube channel. This is where any speaker who dreams of fame can have their dreams fulfilled potentially with views in the millions.

The only time I had experienced views in the millions was back in the late eighties when I had appeared on live TV across the UK while co-hosting a young gardeners' slot on BBC1's lunchtime magazine programme, Daytime Live. In those days, with only four channels to choose from, TV programmes regularly had viewing figures of over five million, even at lunchtime. My mother was so proud. My schoolmates hated me.

TEDxBasel speakers had been told to expect to wait up to six weeks before videos of our talks could be edited and uploaded onto the YouTube channel. In my impatience to share my talk with family back in the UK, I obtained a download of the live-streamed version from an acquaintance who knows how to do that kind of thing.

A month passed and there was excitement building up amongst the speakers. We'd had little word from the organisers but there was a rumour that some of the talks would be uploaded in the next couple of weeks.

It was not until the beginning of July that I was contacted by Harrison, asking if he and Jane could meet with me to discuss my talk. When we met in the café at the top of Switzerland's tallest building, I was relaxed in giving them my candid feedback about the event: what I thought worked well as a speaker and what could be improved for next time.

I knew that my friend O'Patrick had also given them his feedback as an audience member and TED enthusiast. Having been to other TED events, he wanted to offer some suggestions. Always fair in his assessments, he had even drawn up one of his "mind-maps" showing what he thought worked well and how the event could be improved in the future. When Jane asked, he had shared with them how he'd witnessed my experience as a speaker: he knows me better than most, as we've worked closely together for 15 years.

In the café, I sensed an abrupt change in the conversation when we spoke about the experience I'd had through the process. I felt Jane and Harrison were about to land something big on me. They did.

"We are going to edit out the section where you said bullshit", Harrison announced.

"Do I have a say in the matter?", I asked.

"No", said Jane sharply. "It's not negotiable."

Again they cited the reasons of showing it to their classes at school and losing views from American audiences. I was clearly not satisfied with this and asked them to reconsider. Jane was adamant, while Harrison suggested we all sleep on the matter. We parted amicably but I left with a sense of discord emerging. Jane seemingly wasn't happy that I had disobeyed her on The Big Day and used that word without her permission on her stage.

I followed up immediately with an e-mail – as I'm wont to do – in the hope that they would reconsider:

Good to see you both today, hope you enjoyed the tower view.

I hope we were able to shed light on the perceptions and emotions surrounding O'Patrick's comments. He was only saying what he saw, even if I didn't see what he saw in the thick of things. And I really did appreciate all the work you put in.

I'd ask you to please sleep on the censorship issue. I really would not be happy to lose THAT word. Rory Sutherland

⬜another TED speaker⬜used the word "shite" in his TED talk and still got 2.7 million views...

Best wishes,

Peter

I slept on the matter and the next day I thought I would offer a compromise: a bleep. That should please everyone. I sent off another e-mail that morning:

Dear Jane, Harrison,

I have reflected on our conversation yesterday regarding my use of "that word".

I certainly don't regret using it on the day and if we did it all over again tomorrow, I would use it again. As I explained to you yesterday, I certainly didn't disregard your advice not to use it. I tried not using it in my many rehearsals and for me, it just didn't work as well. So I had to use it on the day for the desired impact. Once. I make no apologies for that.

My TED talk was written for adults and not with an audience of children in mind. I think that the next time you invite speakers, if you want us to design our talk for children, then perhaps the outcome would be slightly different. I also don't agree with your point about American audiences. They are adults too, and if they don't like the use of that word, they can turn it off and watch something else. Something with people shooting each other perhaps.

What I do object to strongly is the heavy-handed use of censorship of something like this when representing an organisation that promotes the spread of ideas. I find it totally contrary to the spirit of TED itself.

However, I do concede that you have the ultimate decision and, as you told me in no uncertain terms yesterday, that is "not negotiable".

I would still like my idea to spread, which was my original intention when first getting involved. So I am willing to allow you to bleep out the "shit". Not the "bull", just the "shit". Please use a bleep, not an edit. By doing this, the impact is not reduced too significantly and you could still play it to a child. I look forward to seeing the final video published very soon I hope.

All the best

Peter

On reflection, my comment about watching something with people shooting each other was somewhat inappropriate, but my point was that there are far worse things that anyone can watch at the click of a mouse than someone saying the word "bullshit" in a TED talk. Indeed, President Trump hasn't been prudish with his choice of words since entering office.

Chapter 22: How to organise a Short Notice/Impromptu Speech

This chapter looks at what strategies a speaker might use in preparing the speech. Usually, the time, given to organise, is equal in length to the speech, often two, three or four minutes. It is prepared away from the auditorium. So the speaker needs some simple strategies to allow for the short preparation time. Often, the speaker is given a choice of topics. Adds a further dilemma. which one will the speaker choose.

How to get organised:

Remember it is a speech. It needs an introduction which grabs the audience's attention. It needs a body that develops one main point. As a general rule, you need three minutes to develop one point. Lastly, it needs a conclusion that links to your opening.

Your speech needs a theme to link it together. Decide on it quickly. Having a theme and a good opening allows your subconscious to work ahead of what you are actually saying. Therefore, your speech will seem fluent and well thought out to your audience.

It is best if it contains personal experiences because no one knows your story so any omissions or mistakes don't exist. Therefore, it is easy to create an emotional appeal to get your audience involved.

Strategies you could use:

There are many you might use. The first group of suggestions would be useful particularly for beginners. They are:

How, when, where, why, what, who about your topic

Tracing your theme through the past; the present and the future

Looking at the theme through the eyes of a child, a teenager and an adult

By relating it to current events

Looking at it locally, regionally, nationally and internationally

Personal story

The following suggestions would give the more experienced greater scope to show their prowess. They are:

Social, political, economic

Personal beliefs

Yes/no argument

Cause and effect

Failure and success

Relate your speech to current affairs

Remember to stress that the title of the speech must draw the student to the theme he/she might develop which should then lead to the selection of one of the above strategies. If the mind clogs up, then the student should quickly revert to a personal story or experience.

Finally, might I just share with you my own experience in a short notice speaking competition? I had to select a title out of hat. All I got was a piece of paper with a dot in the middle of it. At first, I thought it was a mistake but I was already losing planning time. Therefore, being a Maths teacher and recently introducing the concept of a point, I discussed this issue as the theme in my speech. I related the difference between a point in geometry and in normal everyday speech. The piece of paper I got for the speech was, in fact, a dud but the speech still succeeded. It just showed a mistake can be the makings of a good, short notice speech.

Chapter 23: Advertisements & Audience Analysis

Nike Bahr

Topic: A practical application of audience analysis

Learning Objectives: By the end of this activity, students will have applied the theoretical main factors of audience analysis to popular print advertisements. Students will have practiced their analytical skills by discussing the marketing strategies of print advertisements.

Description of Activity: Teaching students theoretical frameworks can often prove itself to be difficult. While they confirm their understanding after hearing explanations, the required application afterwards does not usually support that claim. In public speaking classes, we can observe this issue on a regular basis since students have not usually dealt with materials discussed. A topic which is highly important but falls into this exact category is audience analysis: An important part of public speaking, students traditionally have not explicitly interacted with this concept as far as they are aware. Students may not immediately recognize it, but they in fact deal with it every day! Every advertisement they see is targeted to a certain audience. This activity taps into students' indirect knowledge of audience engagement, and is an enjoyable way to deepen their understanding of theoretical frameworks.

Materials needed:

Paper copies of print advertisements (cut outs from magazines or online print outs). One ad per group.

Something that works very well are ad campaigns for candy. Students will be familiar with the brand and companies usually have creative marketing strategies (see Oreo, Sour Patch Kids, Reese's, etc.).

Paper copies of student instructions (see below)

Optional: Digital versions of the advertisements in a slide show

Assignment time:

15 minutes of group work

30 minutes of debrief / discussion

Instructions for Instructor: This activity is targeted to reinforce concepts of audience analysis. Hence, before you can do this activity with your class, you need to introduce said concepts and the theoretical framework you feel is necessary to construct a solid basis for audience analysis. Once you have done so, this activity is easily adjusted to fit your students' needs to gain better practical experience in audience analysis. To ensure that students see the reasoning behind dealing with advertising in a public speaking class, I usually have a short discussion at the beginning of class and ask students what advertisement they remember the most. This question usually results in discussions about jingles, colors, occurrence, and establishes a nice bridge towards a conversation about the key concepts of audience analysis. You can use this point to reinforce knowledge about audience analysis that was established prior to the activity. Topics for a class discussion here may include: How do ads target specific groups/demographics? How do you get engaged looking at an ad? Once you feel students have sufficiently engaged in the discussion and have remembered the key concepts you introduced, begin the activity.

Tell students to get into groups of 3-4 people; for this activity, smaller groups are more beneficial. Once your students have gotten together, hand each group a paper copy of an advertisement (a different one per group) and of the student instructions.

Give students about 15 minutes to discuss their advertisement, make notes and prepare a short presentation of their findings.

Ask each group to present their findings. If you put each advertisement on a slide and project it in front of the class, the groups can stay seated which usually creates bigger comfort and avoids the shuffling of presenting in front of the class.

Initial class discussion for every advertisement/debrief. If they don't talk, you can ask the following questions:

How does this advertisement speak to you?

Would you buy this? Why/why not?

What is most notable for you?

What could they have done better?

Instructions for Students: You have received a print advertisement. Make sure everyone in your group is familiar with the product this ad tries to sell you and that everyone has a chance to take a look at it.

All set? Great! You have about 15 minutes to discuss the following questions and to prepare a presentation for the rest of the class.

Tip: Make notes of your discussion!

Questions for discussion:

What are the demographics of the targeted audience in this ad?

What strategies are used to engage this audience?

What are the values you can find in this ad?

What interests does it address?

Necessary background: Basic understanding of audience analysis

Variations: None

Debrief: Ask your students to reflect on the following:

How can we apply this to public speaking?

Why is audience analysis important for speech writing?

Chapter 24: Learn from Others' Mistakes

You must have heard the advice: "Learn from your mistakes…" Well we can just modify it a little: "Learn from others' mistakes too…" And it still holds true. Some of the great names who haven't been that popular in the art of public speaking are listed below. We can note down their shortcomings just to be sure that we don't make the same errors!

Francesco Schettino: His example makes us realize that effective speaking and listening skills are not only important for our career or professional life, it might become a vital issue in our personal and in times of emergency. It might be a matter of life and death and your communication skills will be hugely tested. In the middle of a crisis, efficiently listening and effectively speaking is vital as the race against time is on. Due to his ineffective communications, 32 lives were lost. He couldn't even save them by the lifeboats that were available.

Todd Aiken & Richard Mourdock: You have to understand that when you are addressing an audience, what you say might have repercussions – positive or negative, depending on what you say. So be cautious as to what you say. Aiken made the mistake of making remarks on the topic of "legitimate rape" which fired up the emotions of the masses and led to his failure in the political run. On the other hand Mourdock made the mistake of claiming about "God intending for rape to happen", a sensitive topic that the masses didn't agree with him.

Bashar Al-Assad: The president of Syria is a contradicting person. While his words and principle might have inspired many, his actions and the current condition of his country shows that his words in an interview is not what he practices. This non-alignment of the words and action will lead to the audience losing faith or trust in you.

John McAfee: The computer programmer was also the presidential candidate from the Libertarian Party of the US. His is the first anti-virus that went commercial with the McAfee name. Popular for various things, communication wasn't his strength and this was seen when he was requested to go for questioning on the event of the murder of his neighbor, he went into hiding. This is another case of non-alignment of words and actions. While he took to secretly took to complaining to the media, he clearly avoided facing the officials.

Hope Solo: The two-time Olympic gold medalist and a World Cup gold medalist, Solo is regarded as one of the top female goal keepers in the world. But all these success and victories is overshadowed by her arrogance and lack of humility. Success alone cannot sustain if the people around you doesn't applaud your victory.

Due to her ineffective communication skills, she misses out on a lot of progress in her due to her careless attitude. And once the audience perceives that you don't care about them, they will return the feeling similarly.

Joe Biden: The vice president of US smiles when he delivers his speech and is cordial in the way he speaks, but the smiles are more calculated and inappropriate than natural, it kills the purpose of the smile. Like mentioned earlier, these small attributes that sets or destroys the presentation or speech. Being natural is necessary to set the conversational tone, which will make the audience comfortable to listen to you.

Mark Pincus: The CEO of Zynga exhibits some attributes which are essentially non examples of effective communications. Likability is an attribute you need to earn from your audience and it depends on how you present yourself and your point. Crossed arms, a smug smile and an uninviting tone set the wrong image of the speaker. It shows that the speaker is arrogant. The audience will not be able to connect to him. Also, the using of technical vocabulary and complex terminologies costs him his audience, simplifying the message is something he needs to look into. They say that his communication destroyed his credibility, which is very true.

Ryan Lochte: The eleven-time Olympics medalist has accomplished a lot in his professional life but he is another example of lack of humility on our list. A monotonous voice, with quite a bit of fumbling gives the impression that he is struggling with what to say or rather trying to recall some memorized speech, which dims the celebratory mood of the fans. When it comes to endorsing and representing brands, he wouldn't be an ideal candidate for it as looks along cannot take him far.

David Axelrod: The chief strategist for Obama's campaigns is now the senior advisor to the president. Cautious as to what he says is something he has to work on. And in the eagerness to put his point forward, he forgot to relate and understand the audience. So he came across as an argumentative and defensive which is not a pretty image to give your audience.

Scott Forstall: Success has a lot to do with your communication skills which includes both speaking and listening. This is something this software engineer needs to understand especially since he was heading the software development team for the iPad and iPhone. He was known for not getting along well with his colleagues or seniors. His lack of understanding that to build a software for the world, he needs to understand and accept what the world wants. And this led to his fall.

These are some of the non-examples of effective communication and the consequences of lack of good communication skills and like mentioned earlier, it cost some their career and for some it damaged their reputation. Learning from these mistakes will help you avoid similar shortcomings in your own path.

Searching the YouTube for videos on these people can also be a good idea. It will give you a chance to empathize with the audience and their feelings when the speaker isn't being effective in conveying the intended message.

Chapter 25: Beginning With The Basics: An Essential Primer Kit for Public Speaking

Before we talk about how to spin a yarn that captivates your audience, it's important to lay some groundwork for public speaking in general. If you're already an experienced public speaker, you may find portions of this chapter somewhat redundant, but I highly recommend that you give it good skim regardless.

On the other hand, if you're new to public speaking, this chapter contains critical knowledge that can instantly take your performance to the next level. Don't miss out on these five public speaking tips for a professional-quality performance.

Public Speaking Pro Tip #1: Know Your Audience Like You Know Yourself, Then Speak to Them (In)Directly

Even the giants of the public speaking industry—Tony Robbins, Dan Kennedy, Zig

Ziglar—would have their effectiveness greatly diminished if they were thrust before a crowd that's incompatible with their message or speaking style.

For the rest of us—those without decades of performing experience underneath our belts—a performance not tailored to our specific audience can be an absolute disaster.

So before you so much as consider the overall message of your speech, first consider your audience. Consider them very well.

Who are they? What's a day like in their shoes? What's the first thing they think about in the morning, and the last thing they think about at night? These aren't hypothetical questions. Really ask them to yourself. Even better, ask them to a person who represents your audience.

Then, begin to ask yourself more abstract things about your audience. Things such as:

What moves them? What makes them uncomfortable? What makes them happy? What would they need to hear for their eyes to swell up with tears of pride? For their skin to break out in goose pimples? For a shiver to run down their spine?

There's no universal answer to these questions, just like there's no universal audience, just like there's no universal message.

That's why you must tailor your speech accordingly. First profile your audience. Then decide exactly what it is you want to tell them—your speech's overall message. Make sure it suits them. Then summarize this into one concise sentence. Then trim that sentence down to core as much as humanly possible. Make it stupid simple.

Take these examples:

The stupid simple message of MLK's I Have a Dream speech is "Equality for all races in society."

The stupid simple message of Reagan's Tear Down This Wall speech is "End this oppressive regime."

Watch these famous speeches, and notice how each of their messages is relayed—at the peak moment of the speech—through potent metaphors.

A dream is a powerful word that's embroiled with positive feelings. A dream is more than a goal, it's a dream. It's a worthy ideal, a lofty proposition, and usually something far from reach. And yet, King's true message called for an immediate change in society. He only used the word symbolically.

Reagan's metaphor was much more specific: The Berlin Wall, a powerful token of an oppressive regime's toll on civil liberties. But at the same time, the wall itself was of little consequence.

It could have been bulldozed the day prior, but with the oppressive policies it represented still in place, the fact that the wall itself was now rubble would have meant nothing. Reagan used the wall to blast the policies.

Human beings have a strong affinity for metaphors like this. We're moved by symbolic representation because symbols affect us on intellectual and emotional level.

Why, after all, are metaphors so frequently employed in nearly all forms of communication? From causal conversation to pre-written speeches, from heated arguments to structured debates? It's because metaphors are stories in miniature. And stories speak to us symbolically.

With the matter of your audience and message both well in hand, you can confidently set your mind upon the how. That is to say, the task of how to deliver your message as effectively as possible.

Well, the most tried and true way to do that is through symbolic representation— storytelling—the subject of this book.

Public Speaking Pro Tip #2: Practice Creates Confidence, So Practice, Practice, Practice

The fear of public speaking is as natural as the fear of heights, the fear of enclosed spaces, and the fear of vaguely human-shaped figures leaping out from the shadows and attacking.

In other words, the fear of public speaking is a deep-set, DNA-bound, instinctual fear. Thankfully, the fear of public speaking can be greatly diminished through good old fashioned practice and preparation.

They say practice makes perfect. Well, when public speaking is concerned, my motto has always been: forget about perfect. Do yourself a favor and throw perfect out the window right this instant. There's no such thing as a perfectly delivered speech.

Even the most skilled and practiced public speaker trips over his tongue, loses his place, or fails to "hit the high note" of his speech from time to time. The pros gladly accept that these things will happen. It takes the weight of inhuman expectations off their shoulders, and it lets them perform more naturally.

No, when it comes to public speaking, practice is great because practice creates confidence.

It goes without saying that the sooner you begin rehearsing, the more confident you'll be when the day of your speech arrives. I've even worked with talented speakers who begin rehearsing a speech before they've even finished writing it!

That may seem counter-intuitive, but the act of verbalizing your speech before its finalized—and thus, hearing your ideas breathed into life out loud—helps refine your message as you write it.

Public Speaking Pro Tip #3: Speech Writing Has No Rules, Only Guidelines

On that note, a brief side tangent on speech writing in general. If you were drafting a novel, the previous paragraph's advice would be considered blasphemous to most well-studied writers. When drafting an essay or unspoken story, the conventional wisdom is to not edit as you write.

But speechwriting is a realm where conventional wisdom rarely applies.

Understand that a speech is perhaps the most profound and personal form of communication in the world. Unless you have a team of speech-writers and speech-coaches in the wing to craft your performance for you, your speech is a unique message from within—a well-polished product of your one-of-a-kind outlook and mentality.

When writing a speech, you really have to trust what you're doing because your speech is literally an expression of you.

To quote the great writer Steven Pressfield in his book, Do The Work:

"Trust the soup."

Trust the what? Here's what Pressfield means by this. When you sit down to draft your speech, and suddenly you find that your soul starts to pore out of your body and onto the page—all before you can so much as summarize your idea in bullet points format...just let it out. Let it flow. Don't fight it.

Understand that your subconscious mind is at work for you constantly in ways you're not aware. That's not airy fairy guru pep-talk, that's proven psychological fact. So don't resist whatever bubbles up from your subconscious when go to write your speech. Trust the soup.

Likewise, if you sit down to draft your speech and find that your story comes to you one chunk at a time, each block in demand of fine-tuning before the next block arrives: go with that as well. But in this regard don't sabotage yourself with the toxic myth of writer's block.

Push through the mental barriers until your speech is finished. To paraphrase another line from Pressfield's work: diamonds aren't scooped out of the sand with a shovel. They're very difficult to harvest.

All of that being said, when it comes to telling stories there's a certain structure— a loose set of guidelines, really—that humans find universally appealing and relatable. You'll learn how to fit your spoken stories into this structure during the next chapter.

Public Speaking Pro Tip #4: Emotional Cadence and Cantor – The Unspoken Subtext of Your Speech

If you yourself don't get emotionally involved in your speech, how can you expect your audience to?

A good speech delivery is a bit like a rollercoaster. It has peaks and valleys, anticipation and momentum. All of these things are communicated through your tone of voice, your pacing, and your overall body language.

The good news is: if you're speaking from the heart, these things should all come to you rather naturally. Most novices' problems with performing stem from inhibiting themselves too much.

Do yourself a favor and look up Charlie Chaplin's performance of "The Greatest Speech Ever Told" from his 1940 film, The Great Dictator. Hear the way his volume rises and falls; the way his rate of speaking gains pace as his message comes to head. Hear the way his voice quakes and falters during certain painful moments.

Don't get me wrong, you definitely don't need to reduce yourself to a blubbering mess on stage in order to deliver your message effectively. But you should strive to convey some level of personal vulnerability to your audience.

When you expose your inner workings to your audience, they become receptive to your message on the same sort of deeply personal wavelength.

Chapter 26: THE ROLE OF THE SPEAKER IN SUCCESSFUL PUBLIC SPEAKING

The speaker, more than any other part of the public speaking process determines to the largest extent the success or failure of public speaking.

The speaker is the carrier of the idea, which he wants to communicate to his audience. Though he may have command over the subject matter, yet a failure in the other personal factors can mar the whole process. This chapter therefore, more than anything else seeks to discuss how as a speaker you can employ other personal factors effectively to enhance your chances of success in public speaking.

We shall look at these personal factors under the following: Personality, Appearance, and Competence.

Appearance

I. DRESSING

II. HYGIENE

III. POSTURE

IV. MANNERISM

Personality

I. SOCIABILITY

II. AGREEABLENESS

III. ADJUSTABILITY

IV. CONSCIENTIOUSNESS

v. Intellectual Openness

Competence

I. KNOWLEDGEABLE

II. SKILFUL

III. CONFIDENT

Appearance

Appearance is very important in public speaking because the audience sees your outward appearance before they hear what you have to say. If your outside puts them off before you open your mouth to speak, both your purpose and message would be a failure. As a public speaker therefore, you must take your time to package yourself in a way that can win you the admiration of your audience and their eagerness to listen to you.

181

You may want to consider the following areas in packaging yourself for a positive impact on your audience; Dressing, Hygiene, Posture and Mannerism.

a. Dressing:

Dress neatly, attractively and be well groomed. The consciousness of being well dressed heightens one's self respect, increases self-confidence, and increases faith in one's self. When you have a look of success, you find it easier to think success and to achieve success. Such is the effect of clothes on you the wearer.

What effect do your clothes have on your audience?

If you as a male speaker, appear in a baggy trousers, shapeless coat and footwear, fountain pen and pencil peeping out of your breast pocket, a newspaper or a smoking pipe and a can of tobacco sticking out of the sides of your garment your audience will not take you serious to deserve their attention.

Alternatively, as a woman with an ugly, bulging purse with your slip showing, you will notice that the audience has as little respect for you as you have for your own appearance. They will assume that the mind is as sloppy as the unkempt hair, unpolished shoes, or the bulging handbag.

b. Hygiene

Any time you are to appear before an audience, remember that all eyes are going to be on you like cameras with zoom lenses. Your personal hygiene is therefore paramount in determining the level of acceptance you receive from the audience. As you stand before any audience, you must know that you're under the scrutiny of their eyes from the crown of your hair to the sole of your feet. Your hair must be well kept. As a man, you should cut your hair regularly and trim your beard nicely. Your oral hygiene must be observed strictly, as you are going to be standing before people and interacting with people. Brush your teeth and use a mouthwash to remove any unfriendly odour from your mouth. Also remember to take care of any offensive body odour as well.

c. Posture:

If a picture is worth a thousand words, then body language in public speaking is worth at least a thousand dollars! That may sound a little corny, but the bottom line is that people do business with people they like and people with whom they feel comfortable.

In business communications, over half (about 55%) of our total communicated message is sent through our body language. Twenty-two percent (22%) is the tone of voice we use, and only 7 percent (7%) is portrayed through the actual words we use.

Seven Seconds to a Positive Impression

Have you ever met someone and instantly said to yourself, "I don't know why, but I really like that person," or "There's something about that guy that bugs me."

You have just formed an impression of the other person. Most of our first impressions are subconscious; we don't even know we are making them. We only know that we have an overall, general feeling about a person.

Eight Subconscious Impressions That Happen Within Seven Seconds

Here are eight opinions people generally make of you within the first seven seconds of meeting you:

i. How much money you make

ii. How much education you've had

iii. How much you can be trusted

iv. Your personality style and how agreeable you are

v. How confident you are

vi. How intelligent you are

vii. What your work ethic is

viii. How dependable and accountable you are

Wait a minute! How can someone make all these decisions about someone in the first seven seconds? Good question. Let us

185

talk about some tips to make a good impression in the first seven seconds.

The Walk

The first thing people notice about you is your walk. If you keep three things in mind, you will be on your way to projecting a more professional image:

· Stand upright. Hold your head up. This shows how confident you are.

· Do not hide your hands. Do not put them in your pockets or hold them behind your back. Why? Because if your hands are not showing it sends a subliminal message that you cannot be trusted, that you have something to hide.

· Walk with a purpose and with enthusiasm. This shows your personality and confidence. No one likes to see someone trudging up to them, head down, eyes diverted.

Personality:

Personality contributes to business success than superior intelligence. Personality —with the exception of preparation −is probably the most important factor in public speaking. In eloquent speaking, it is manner that wins not words.

Personality is the whole combination of the whole person: spiritual, mental, and physical together with traits, tendencies, temperaments, attitudes, mental disposition, vigour, experience, training etc.

Personality is determined by inheritance and environment, and is extremely difficult to alter or improve. Yet through thoughtful effort, we can strengthen it to some extent and make it more forceful and more attractive.

Competence:

In your role as a public speaker, it is important that you are both knowledgeable in your subject matter, skilled in speaking techniques and confident in your presentation. Your ability to speak effectively is enhanced with knowledge, skill, and confidence resulting in greater audience interest. You gain knowledge through study and skill through application of what you learned.

Knowledge and Skill

Being a knowledgeable speaker means you are well informed about subject matters and speaking techniques. A speaker who has insufficient knowledge does not know what he or she is talking about and does not know how to make an effective presentation.

Being skilled in speaking means, you have mastered speaking techniques and are able to deliver a speech in an effective manner.

Knowledge and skill are part of the natural progression from good health, excellence, value, and honour.

Being confident means you have mastered stage fright and conquered nervousness in your delivery process.

Importance and Benefits of Knowledge, Skill and Confidence

It is much easier to give a speech if you thoroughly know the subject matter and are skilled in speaking techniques. Lack of knowledge can result in anxiety and embarrassment. The audience responds better to a knowledgeable speaker.

A speaker who is skilled in platform techniques will know how to deliver a good speech in various circumstances and be able to adjust to unexpected changes. A skilled speaker can often overcome a lack of knowledge through his or her speaking ability.

Confidence, esteem and audience appreciation are some of the rewards from being knowledgeable and skilled. If you set a goal of giving a speech to the best of your ability and you succeed in that, you get the sense of achievement and confidence. It is a good feeling when you complete a difficult speech. It can increase your confidence in being able to attempt tasks that are more challenging.

How to Become Knowledgeable

The way to gain knowledge in your subject matter and speaking techniques is to observe, study, and read. Speakers are known to be perceptive observers and readers. There are lots of books on speaking and presentation techniques, as well as those on the various subjects and topics for the speeches.

Applying what you have learned and analysing the results of your work are also good ways to establish your skills.

The public speaker should be knowledgeable in his or her subject matter and skilled in speaking techniques. Skilful and knowledgeable speaking increases your confidence and results in greater audience interest. You can gain knowledge through study and skill through application of what you learned.

Character:

Character and the Public Speaker

In your role as a public speaker, whether professionally, on the job or for enjoyment, it is important to have good character. Being honourable and honest in the work you do and in your relations to others is essential in speaking and in your profession. Having an honourable character also provides you with personal benefits, can enhance your career, and lend source credibility to your message.

Having character means that you are honourable, honest, have integrity, are reliable and responsible. On the opposite end of the spectrum, there are people who lie, cheat, or steal. They may also be lazy, unreliable, or inconsiderate of others.

It is obvious that honesty and integrity are important in the workplace, as well as from the speaking lectern. The same is true for reliability and other forms of character. The public speaker must be ethical and conscientious in his or her activities. This is especially important when making presentations to a group. Having an honourable character is a natural progression from being healthy, skilled, excellent, and valuable to the audience.

Importance and Benefits of Good Character

Being a person and speaker of high character is important to your relationship with other people, your career, and your own self-worth. If you are known as an honest and honourable speaker, and a person who is reliable and responsible, those with whom you deal will respect you. Your speaking audience, as well as your fellow workers and supervisors will trust you, know they can depend on you, and want to hear what you have to say. People certainly don't want to listen to a speech from someone who lies, steals or is immoral.

Another important factor is that being an honourable public speaker gives you greater self-esteem. You feel good about yourself. Finally, there is the religious aspect of being honest, moral, and ethical.

Your actions determine what people think of you and establish your reputation. They also determine how others will respond to what you do and say. The way to have character is to make sure that you are always honest, honourable, and forthright. Make sure there is no implication of dishonesty in any form.

You should also seek to be considerate of others and conscientious in your public speaking. This doesn't mean that you have to be perfect, but it does mean that you are trying to be someone of high character.

A public speaker needs to be honest and reliable. Your reputation affects how people deal with you. Having good character results in others respecting you and increases your own self-esteem. Having character requires a constant effort.

Conclusion

Thank you again for downloading this book!

I hope this book was able to help you to figure out how to overcome your fear of speaking in public and move on to making presentations with confidence.

The next step is to put these tips and strategies into motion. With just the right preparation and practice, anyone can overcome their fear of public speaking and become confident speakers.

I challenge you and encourage you to pick at least one step or idea from this book and take action on it immediately. Whether it's to sign up for social activity, or research your nearest Toastmasters club, or volunteer to do a talk or to run a meeting. Pick something and take action on it now.

Thank you and good luck!

CPSIA information can be obtained
at www.ICGtesting.com
Printed in the USA
BVHW061542261222
654958BV00016B/796

9 781989 990100